SUMMARY OF

MEDICAL MEDIUM

LIVER

RESCUE

ANSWERS TO ECZEMA, PSORIASIS, DIABETES, STREP, ACNE, GOUT, BLOATING, GALLSTONES, ADRENAL STRESS, FATIGUE, FATTY LIVER, WEIGHT ISSUES, SIBO & AUTOIMMUNE DISEASE

BY
Anthony William

Proudly Brought To You By
Knowledge Crave

Table of Contents

EXECUTIVE SUMMARY

Medical science and research are yet to truly understand or even scratch the surface of what causes many of the health issues currently plaguing humans. This book, "Liver Rescue" is not another addition to the many recycled theories and practices out there.

Anthony William seeks to educate the reader on steps to take towards understanding various disorders as well as how to embark on recovering from them. He does this by emphasizing the need for us to take good care of our livers. Many of the health conditions we encounter can be traced to this organ. A sluggish and contaminated liver opens up the way for toxins in it to enter our bloodstream and flow into the rest of our bodies.

Anthony takes us through the peacekeeping role the liver plays. Even though we do not pay the liver much attention, the organ is responsible for causing or eliminating health conditions such as diabetes, depression, eczema, psoriasis, adrenal problems, etc. All these are liver-related problems, and we can tackle them by giving the liver what it needs to function correctly.

Anthony William's Liver Rescue Morning and Liver Rescue 3:6:9 plan is the perfect program to restore the liver to its normal state of effectively performing over 2,000 chemical functions in our body. He also offers unique meditation techniques that are soothing, relaxing, and beneficial to the liver.

Rest assured, after reading this book, you'll be making some necessary and healthy lifestyle changes.

CHAPTER 1: WHAT YOUR LIVER DOES FOR YOU

Key Takeaways:

- *Our livers are seemingly insignificant but vital organs of our body.*

- *The liver has many functions that protect and preserve the body.*

- *Our livers are failing and must be rescued.*

- *A healthy liver corrects every abnormality in other parts of the body.*

- *Medical science has discovered only a meager amount of the liver's ability.*

Some things become real to us only when we see for ourselves. Such is the case with a soon-to-be parent in the ultrasound lab viewing the image of a growing fetus in the womb. At that moment, the reality sets in with full force. Similarly, getting to know our liver better will bring us into the reality of its wonder-working abilities.

The liver is not as popular as other parts of the body. It isn't given much importance in our school syllabuses either, unlike the brain or the heart. But beyond education, the liver's abilities are more hidden than that of other organs. For instance, we can quickly detect symptoms of brain illnesses or feel our heart beat abnormally after a jog.

However, the liver seems to be more like a ghost, not easily seen. It remains a mystery to many, yet holds the explanation for several health complaints. Many times, we have wrongly blamed the heart, gut, genes or the thyroid for several chronic illnesses. While these organs are also vital, the cause of these health problems is usually a failing liver. So, why is the liver so important in the grand scheme of things? With over 2,000 vital functions, it is a significant protector and preserver of your body.

Hence, the need to take care of your liver. This seemingly insignificant organ is the key to taking care of all other aspects of your well-being. However, our livers are not getting better by the day. Beyond liver cancer, cirrhosis, and hepatitis, this vital organ can also serve as catalyst to diverse other conditions and diseases; It must be given utmost attention in our lives. Saving our liver from the trouble it's headed for is equivalent to having a balanced blood sugar, optimum blood pressure, monitored weight, and a younger and fresher body. A liver in good health will take care of the issues of stress and rapid aging. Therefore, the consequences of ignoring this vital organ are life-threatening.

Our livers are in trouble because of exposure to toxins in our environment. They suffer when our blood gets contaminated with antibiotics, chronic dehydration, viral and bacterial waste matter, excess fat from unhealthy foods, etc. About 900 out of 1000 people have a failing liver and it's worse because majority of these people have no idea. These folks are not completely at fault. Medical science in itself has barely scratched the surface on identifying all the roles the liver plays or how many health troubles and conditions have their roots in a hurting liver. This ignorance places more work on our organs as they have to work way beyond reasonable. Many times when we experience brain fog, fatigue, weight gain, high blood pressure, acne, or anxiety, it is a sign that our livers crying out for help. In other words, we can safely say that a healthy liver would eradicate illness of all forms in the human population.

With such massive importance, we would take liver education even more seriously if we uncovered its full abilities. However, we are mostly ignorant and keep straining the delicate organ. Our lifestyle of liver abuse often begins at a young age and lasts as long as the doctor is yet to give a diagnosis of liver failure or something similar.

College students upset their livers with drugs, alcohol, and caffeine. Working class individuals overburden theirs to get jobs done and meet absurd deadlines. Surprisingly, with some of us, our form of abuse involves eating the liver of other animals. When we invest in this liver education, we will learn how it is responsible for processing fat and protecting the pancreas, storing glucose and glycogen, storing vitamins and minerals, disarming and detaining harmful materials, screening and filtering blood, and even guarding our bodies with its personalized immune system.

CHAPTER 2: YOUR ADAPTOGENIC LIVER PROCESSING FAT AND PROTECTING YOUR PANCREAS

Key Takeaways:

- *Your liver is the most adaptogenic organ in your body.*

- *Your liver rapidly performs different chemical functions for your body.*

- *Your liver breaks down fat and converts it into an energy source for your body.*

- *Your liver releases a bile composition to process the fats in your diet.*

- *Extra fats are stored in your lymphatic system.*

If you thought your brain was highly adaptive, then you need to see your liver in action. Your liver is the only organ in your body that is genuinely adaptogenic.

There's no situation a healthy liver can't adapt to. The brain may have adaptive abilities but not in all cases. This is evident with a new employee who takes months if not years to understand a particular concept or process. For some people, they may never be able to wrap their heads around a thing even after asking a ton of questions, but this is not the case with the liver. It adapts and switches roles at top speed to perform different chemical functions.

A healthy liver will generate heat to warm you when you're cold and in turn, cool you when you get hot. Your liver stops excess water from diluting your blood composition by absorbing the water like a sponge. It can absorb smoke chemicals in your bloodstream, break down trans fatty acids to keep you safe and even release vaults of adrenaline when you're in danger. Even more interesting is how the liver is a memory bank. It documents your eating habits over the years, remembers that the weekend is pizza time for you and prepares ahead of time. Your liver's memory is trustworthy and reliable. And if there is any change in your eating or lifestyle habits, it adapts accordingly.

Your liver plays a very key role in processing fat. It releases bile to break down fat and converts it into energy for the body. The production of bile is hinged upon your fat intake at every meal. This informs your liver's level of alert. The first level is the Code Green which involves bile composition required for a diet composed of 15 percent or less of fat from healthy sources such as fruits, nuts, dairy, vegetables, and legumes. At this level, the liver produces necessary bile composition at a standard rate. At Code Yellow, the liver has a low-level alert as it raises bile production by 5% when someone's diet is composed of 15% or less of fats from unproductive sources.

Code Orange raises bile levels by 10% when someone's diet is 15-30% fat from healthy sources. When the diet remains at 15-30% fat but comes from unproductive sources, the liver goes into Code Orange-Plus. Here, bile production increases by up to 15-20% . But when bile levels rise by up to 20-25%, it means that the diet consists of 30-40% fat from healthy sources. This is known as Code Red as the liver begins to send out warning signals. Code Red-Plus launches the liver into an all-out adaptogenic phase as it draws on all of its reserves to increase bile production by 50%. This is when the diet is 30% or more fat from unproductive sources. These sources could be foods in a ketogenic diet which are plant protein-based or animal protein-based.

Your liver is a lifesaver. It pays attention to the oxygen levels in your bloodstream to detect whether you're in Code Green, Code Red-Plus, or in between. Oxygen in our blood lowers with more radical fats in our diet. This causes our livers to release bile to break down these fats and thin the blood. The liver also takes up all these responsibilities to protect the pancreas. Your pancreas is a delicate organ that produces the hormone insulin to regulate blood sugar. Excess fat affects your pancreas which makes it produce more and more insulin to the extent of being unable to produce any. This eventually leads to diabetes. However, your liver works tirelessly to protect your body from these excess fats. When your liver can't protect you from excess fat entirely, it delivers the extra fats to the lymphatic system. However, this is not completely pleasant affair as the immune system weakens and white killer cells are unable to battle viruses, bacteria, and toxins. If the fat-filled diet is exchanged for foods like pumpkin, sweet potatoes, squash, zucchini, berries, and other fruits, there will be less insulin resistance and more balanced blood sugar level.

CHAPTER 3: YOUR LIFE-GIVING LIVER: GLUCOSE AND GLYCOGEN STORAGE

Key Takeaways:

- *Your liver stores beneficial nutrients for future body absorption.*
- *Glycogen is broken down to glucose for reabsorption.*
- *Glucose is food for your liver.*
- *All sugar is not the same.*
- *High-fat diets starve the liver of its necessary food.*

Your liver can be likened to a storehouse. It is a preservation center for specific nutrients to be given to your body for absorption. Glucose is one crucial item in this liver storehouse. By storing glucose, conditions such as diabetes are avoided, and your liver helps you stay alive. After running around all day, your liver replenishes your body by releasing the glucose it has stored up. This introduction of sugar prevents you from getting too hypoglycemic or having a pancreas or adrenal crash. Glucose is stored in your liver as glycogen. Your liver also preserves concentrations of other nutrients, hormones, biochemical agents and chemical compounds in this its storage system.

Your liver reabsorbs blood vessels when your brain or thyroid gives the discharge signals. This happens by breaking down glycogen back into glucose or taking an even faster route by releasing readily available glucose that was not stored as glycogen. A well-functioning liver is one that is rich in glucose and glycogen. It fosters blood sugar support on which the body depends. This is what helps marathon runners get to the finish line. Your liver releases all the glucose in its storage to reach the finish line.

The liver very much needs glucose. Your liver thrives on sugar. Right from our first food, breast milk, to our current diet as grown-ups, glucose is instrumental in muscle building, organ development, and maintenance. It is also the fuel your liver uses to support your whole body. However, not all sugars help you. Sweeteners and high-fructose corn syrup are rather bad for our health. But natural sugars from whole foods and the ones got from proper carbohydrates digestion are beneficial. However, grouping these two sets of sugars has led us to feel that all sugar is the same. This is wrong because natural sugars help our livers do its work even better than fats would. The lobules on your liver also feed on glucose. After working all day to sort out everything you're exposed to into "Good" and "Evil," these lobules get hungry and feed on glucose. In other words, hoarding sugars from your body will result in your liver growing weaker and striving to survive.

It would be incredibly wrong to starve the liver of the food it needs. If today's high-fat diets were only fats and protein and didn't include little bits of sugar, the liver would fight and struggle to survive. One of the sources of sugar in these high-fat diets is the avocado. The health benefits of avocados are excellent. They are a combination of fat and valuable sugar and are a healthier source. Avocados give your body the necessary glucose it requires. Hence, carbs and sugar are not the enemies. A diet void of sugar will lead your liver to starvation. Your liver is reliable, and it wants to support you, but you must feed it with what it needs.

CHAPTER 4: YOUR MEDICINAL LIVER: VITAMIN AND MINERAL STORAGE

Key Takeaways

- *A troubled liver causes vitamin and mineral deficiency.*
- *The stomach converts nutrients into usable forms for the body.*
- *Your liver serves as a backup converter when your gut fails.*
- *Digestive disorder is caused by a compromised liver.*
- *Protecting the body from toxins is a crucial job of the liver.*

Cases of vitamin and mineral deficiency are rooted in the fact that your liver is going through some troubles. In other words, the storehouse in your liver is being emptied of its nutrients. This happens when you're not getting such particular nutrients in your diet; the liver begins to run low on vitamins and minerals. A healthy liver can support you with the necessary nutrients. These nutrients were stored after your stomach converted them into usable forms during digestion.

This biochemical conversion enhances the nutrients and conditions it for specific use in your body. The liver also converts them through a chemical process by equipping them with a protective shield and armor. The liver also ensures that they are not destroyed by toxins or affected by excess fat in the bloodstream. These nutrients are finally conveyed into different organs in your body via the blood.

The liver re-dispenses nutrients that the gut provides. However, in cases where the gut cannot absorb, alter and deliver the necessary nutrients, your liver steps up to the role and acts as a backup conversion tool. Your liver then has to do more in the conversion process. This process is known as methylation. When an organ in the body such as the ileum fails to serve well, your liver becomes the go-to guy that keeps your body in place.

Your liver overcompensates for these organs so much that it masks several illnesses and conditions. However, working beyond its capacity will make it too

CHAPTER 5: YOUR PROTECTIVE LIVER DISARMING AND DETAINING HARMFUL MATERIALS

Key Takeaways:

- *The liver prevents many health disasters by processing what we consume.*

- *The liver disarms the ionic charge of harmful substances.*

- *A healthy liver releases detoxifying chemical compounds.*

- *The liver contains a storage bank for vitamins and minerals as well as one for toxins.*

- *Perime cells in the liver help it shapeshift and expand storage bins.*

The capabilities of the liver are sadly underrated. If we realize how beneficial and essential our liver is, then we will appreciate it more. For instance, the liver constantly fights against toxic substances from pesticides in a highly sprayed crop of corn, plastics from a microwaved meal, or the preservatives used in fast food meals. All these are catalysts of potential health disasters, but our livers are ever looking out for us.

We enjoy ice-cream from time to time, not minding that they come from antibiotic-fed cows. The same goes for cocktails containing MSG, dyes and synthetic fruity flavors. Despite the liver's protective function, it sometimes suffers from overworking to keep us danger-free. If anything, we should commend our liver's efforts with a glass of green juice or a meal of steamed potatoes.

The harmful substances we consume such as plastics, pathogens, synthetic pesticides and herbicides, produce a negative ionic charge. They are destructive once they enter into our bloodstream, lymph fluid, and even spinal fluid. This puts nutrients in danger and damages immune system cells as well as red blood cells. These toxins flow towards the liver with their toxic ionic charge. However, a healthy liver that isn't clogged up or stagnant will disarm this charge.

The liver also discharges these toxins' destructive charge in the bloodstream to prevent them from running wild in your body. If not checked by the liver, your body is filled with electricity that can ignite these troublemakers. A struggling liver will suffer to release a meagre amount of the chemical compound that will disarm the havoc-wreaking toxins.

When the release of this chemical compound is impossible, your liver stows away these toxins instead to protect your body. The liver contains a storage facility for glucose, glycogen, vitamins, minerals, and other nutrients as well as a storage facility for harmful materials. However, the storage for harmful toxins arises out of necessity only after the liver cannot get those toxins out of your body. Toxins like petroleum products, pesticides, aspartame, MSG, viral waste matter and such are incredibly damaging.

These toxins that cause the highest risk are hidden away deep inside the liver. They are the closest to your liver's core to protect you. Your liver takes the hit for you while you freely go about enjoying life. All the while, it waits for the moment when it would get the opportunity to cleanse or detox the toxic items. The liver can also undergo storage bins expansions all thanks to the perime cells. These cells help the liver shapeshift to prevent toxins from getting into your bloodstream.

Our livers have worked as a silent organ over the years, withstanding so much trouble and supporting the body. When it gets to the stage of being unable to process fat by storing glucose, glycogen, vitamins and minerals or disarming and containing toxins, it becomes a fatty liver. Then there us the exposure to liver-related problems like gout, diabetes, eczema, psoriasis or cirrhosis. We must, therefore, be responsible for rescuing the liver and bringing it back from the brink before it gets to this emergency stage.

CHAPTER 6: YOUR PURIFYING LIVER SCREENING AND FILTERING BLOOD

Key Takeaways

- *The liver's white blood cells prevent any viruses or bacteria from entering it.*

- *Lobules and Kupffer cells distribute blood to the rest of the body.*

- *The liver buries the most harmful toxins deep within its core.*

- *The liver eliminates toxins through the colon and the kidneys.*

- *The liver replenishes the lobules with adrenaline to contain toxins.*

Your liver is an extremely busy organ. It is filled with good stuff and bad stuff. The good things, being nutrients from the food you eat and the bad consisting of substances such as alcohol, medicines, chemicals, pathogens, and excess adrenaline. Your liver is highly skilled in separating the good stuff from the bad. At the same time, it balances the oxygen in the blood. The liver does this by assigning white blood cells to stand guard at the hepatic portal vein which is the primary gateway to the liver. These cells are on the alert for any virus or bacteria. Blood flows into the liver in smaller vessels where the liver lobules and Kupffer cells sort the helpful stuff and send them on the right way while also running another check for toxins or pathogens that slipped by the white blood cells.

The lobules filter elements coming into the liver while the Kupffer cells act like brooms which the lobules use to sweep the liver clean of bad stuff. Hence, the lobules which are the cleaners will probably get hungry after a while. They feed on glucose and energize the Kupffer cells to do more. It is important that your liver separates the useful material from the harmful because the blood that leaves the liver goes straight into the heart. The blood in the heart has to be clean which is why your liver goes out of its way to battle deadly threats or bury them deep in its core.

The liver also has a screening and filtering process where it gets less-toxic troublemakers out of your body so that it can contain the more dangerous ones. These troublemakers are sent packing via the feces from the colon (sometimes via the bile and gallbladder); urine from the kidneys; or made to run loose in the bloodstream. However, a good and healthy liver will do all it can to prevent this last option.

When the liver weakens, the lobules get overworked and are unable to dispose of troublemakers efficiently. In this case, the troublemakers run wild and journey to the heart. They cycle through the rest of the circulatory system and return to the liver. Eliminating the troublemakers via the colon is the liver's most preferred method. A good liver with sufficient bile will send these toxins packing through the bile duct directly to the intestinal tract or through the hepatic duct to the gallbladder. However, a stagnant and weak liver has no lobules to package the toxins for proper disposal and is also running low on oxygen to use in the delivery process.

The liver also performs a brilliant task of producing a chemical compound that collates the white blood cell guards and uses them as a softening agent on hardened hepatocyte "prison" cell walls. Once the white blood cells enter into the hepatocytes, they eliminate any viruses entrenched in their scar tissue. When the liver gets too defenseless to deal with troublemakers, it sounds an alarm bell and recycles adrenaline for the liver cells and lobules to consume to get the needed strength for containing the toxins.

CHAPTER 7: YOUR HEROIC LIVER THE LIVER'S IMMUNE SYSTEM

Key Takeaways

- *The liver's white blood cells protect your body from pathogens.*
- *The units of the liver's immune system monitor blood flowing into it.*
- *Hepatic artery white blood cells are incredible swimmers.*
- *Hepatic portal vein white blood cells will suffocate if there is limited oxygen.*
- *Liver lymphocytes eliminate EBV cells.*

Our immune system protects us from colds and flu. However, bacteria and viruses go far beneath the surface to wage attacks that are more subtle than these symptoms. The infections present in the liver are responsible for several conditions such as fibromyalgia, multiple sclerosis (MS), rheumatoid arthritis (RA), lupus, Lyme disease, Hashimoto's thyroiditis, shingles and dozens more. However, the liver's network of white blood cells is its immune system that protects your body from pathogens.

The immune system of your liver is made up of six central units unknown to medical science and research. Three of these units monitor the blood entering the liver. They include the hepatic vessel white blood cells, hepatic portal vein white blood cells, and hepatic artery white blood cells. The hepatic vessel white blood cells guard the blood vessels that lead to the portal vein while the hepatic portal vein white blood cells stand guard over the portal vein itself. At the other circulatory entrance to the liver, the hepatic artery white blood cells are stationed where they adapt to entirely different oxygen levels and blood flow.

These hepatic artery white blood cells must swim incredibly fast without worrying about the availability of oxygen. They are real athletes who take a form, unknown to science and research, which affords them movement in an area of rushing blood. It is in contrast to hepatic portal vein white blood cells which are not a fan of speed and can nearly suffocate as a result of lack of oxygen. And if eventually, pathogens escape all these sentries, the lobule white blood cells become the liver's next guard on duty. Their job is to protect the lobules by looking out for bad guys such as the Epstein-Barr Virus (EBV). Unknown to medical science, this virus is the originator of hepatitis A, B, C, D, and E as well as other chronic illnesses caused by liver infections that are medically undetected.

Your liver assigns individual bile duct white blood cells to watch over your bile duct system. These cells are the only components of your liver's immune system that can take on the bile's harsh nature. They stand on the lookout for any element in the bile that may be an agent of liver infection. There are also liver lymphocytes which move around the domain of the outer part of the liver and sometimes also enter the liver if the need be. They eliminate EBV cells attempting to break into the liver through the lymph fluid.

With a weak and overburdened liver, this filtration system is corrupted allowing toxic substances leach into the lymphatic system. We, therefore, have the crucial task of feeding the liver with nutrients and nourishment from mineral-rich foods. This, in turn, strengthens and reinvigorates the liver to do its work which is using the intelligence in its white blood cells to combat bacterium, virus, or even toxins.

CHAPTER 8: SLUGGISH LIVER

Key Takeaways:

- *Pathogens can be passed down from generation to generation.*
- *A sluggish liver is weak and overburdened.*
- *Eczema, psoriasis and acne are symptoms of a sluggish liver.*
- *Sluggish liver causes the liver to lose information stored in its memory.*
- *There are five varieties of sluggish liver.*

You've come to understand that your liver's greatest enemies include viruses, bacteria, molds, pathogenic waste, toxic heavy metals, radiation, DDT and other pesticides, herbicides, fungicides, solvents, pollutants, drugs, medications, alcohol, excess adrenaline, high-fat diets and many more. With time, these harmful substances weaken the liver and render it helpless to protect the human. Many of these pathogens were passed down from generations past. The liver does an excellent job of tackling these bad stuff, and if we don't treat it well, it gets burdened and works sluggishly.

A sluggish liver is a liver at war. It is a gateway into bigger and fiercer battles for the liver. If we could relate with the liver as a person, we'll see the very vital need to give it a break now and then. We get tired and weary while exerting our bodies in our day-to-day activities. At this point of weariness, our output and performance level runs low, and we drag along on completing tasks. The only remedy to this is a good rest. This is exactly the way it is with our livers. Nine out of ten people currently live with a sluggish liver. This condition is to blame for any problem in the liver.

Grave health conditions such as cirrhosis, hepatitis, jaundice, fatty liver, and liver cancer are premeditated upon the sluggish liver. The condition makes the vital organ perform below expectation and makes it unable to protect you. It also paves the way for illnesses to ravage the body. Medical research and science have only documented a few of the symptoms of a compromised liver. What many do not know is that eczema, psoriasis, and even acne come about because of a particular type of overburdened liver. Other symptoms that originate at the liver include mystery high blood pressure, mystery heart palpitations, type

2 diabetes, seasonal affective disorder (SAD), dark under-eye circles, chronic dehydration, varicose veins, weight gain, chemical sensitivities, bloating, as well as constipation. All of these symptoms begin with the liver's inability to work efficiently as a result of a lack of resources.

A sluggish liver should not be thought of as lazy. A sluggish liver works harder in its poor performing state to overcome threats. However, this commendable push can bring it to a stage where it begins to lose its memory. The liver is a memory bank for the body just like the brain and the thyroid, but as harmful substances enter it, it begins to lose the information stored in its memory. One of these hazardous substances is toxic and dirty blood which translates into dark under-eye circles, hot flashes, and liver heat. The liver also has a spasm which it sends out as an anti-sluggish emergency alarm response to receive new, vital energy to overcome stagnancy.

In the events of a sluggish liver, the whole liver doesn't become sluggish all at once. There are five varieties of sluggish liver. Someone could have a sluggish liver in one or even five of all the types. The first variety is the middle of the liver which comes with symptoms such as hot flashes, night sweats, hypoglycemia, and irritability amongst others. The bottom of the liver variety causes tossing and turning at night, as well as hot and cold sensations. The top of the liver variety comes with poor digestion, acid reflux, bloating, corner of lip sores and other mouth sores. When the left lobe of the liver is sluggish, there is nausea, anxiousness, insatiable hunger, and emotional sensitivities. The final variety is the right side of the liver which brings brittle and discolored nails, leg spasms or cramps, or a raw too of the tong fluid.

CHAPTER 9: LIVER ENZYME GUESS TESTS

Key Takeaways

- *Liver enzyme tests are a thing of guesswork in medical societies.*
- *Scans usually do not explain what may be wrong with the body.*
- *Elevated albumin indicates a viral flare.*
- *Elevated bilirubin in the bloodstream indicates a pancreatic or liver condition.*
- *Abnormal enzymes test results signal to us that something is wrong with the liver.*

The mystery of elevated liver enzymes causes medical research and science to believe that it is guesswork and could be fallible or inaccurate. The experts know that something is going on with the liver, but they cannot place their hands on precisely what it is. Even a CT or PET scan, MRI or ultrasound of the liver may not reveal any problems worth taking a more in-depth look into. On the other hand, the scans could reveal visible inflammation, scar tissue, or cystic activity. This could offer medical experts an explanation for the elevated liver enzymes.

However, in most cases, the scans come back with no clues as to what could be the cause. This is where the enzyme test guessing game comes into play. An enzyme test doesn't explain the liver problems that are revealed in scans. Many times, enzyme tests come back standard even when someone has a cyst or scar tissue or a fatty liver. However, an enzyme test still informs doctors and patients that there could be a liver problem. This brings about a change in lifestyle and especially in eating habits. The patient becomes more mindful of his health, and this is a good thing.

Alanine Transaminase (ALT) and Aspartate Aminotransferase (AST) are the two enzymes most commonly tested for in an enzyme test. Others include alkaline phosphatase (ALP) and Gamma-Glutamyl Transpeptidase (GGT). Doctors also conduct blood tests to check for high or low levels of albumin. If it is low, medical research and science believe it signals poor nutrition. If it comes back high, then doctors guess the problem to be a bacterial infection or injury. However, elevated albumin actually indicates a viral flare. Doctors may also come across elevated bilirubin in the bloodstream which could be indicative of a pancreatic problem, a developing liver condition or a bile duct tumor. Medical communities must come to realize that when these tests come back as abnormal, it is a signal that something is wrong with the liver.

Emergency flares from liver enzymes contain information that helps us discover the proteins and chemical compounds that the liver sends as flares. We will be able to decode how certain flares are related to the prevalence of certain insecticides, herbicides, fungicides, or even mercury and aluminum. Enzyme tests offer us clues that the liver is experiencing a hidden condition. However, if these tests are conducted continuously for a period, they will reveal different results. An analysis done today may barely reveal anything, in three days' time, another one may show a drastic elevation, and two days from then, it could all be gone. However, this doesn't discount the usefulness of liver enzyme tests; it is an indication to improve liver health. But it should not be the last probe into the symptoms of liver-related distress.

CHAPTER 10: DIRTY BLOOD SYNDROME

Key Takeaways

- *Our livers adapt to lack of hydration.*
- *A person's genes do not define their constitution.*
- *Dehydration causes blood sugar level to reduce rapidly.*
- *A liter of lemon water in the morning keeps you hydrated all day long.*
- *Toxic substances contaminate the blood as a result of dehydration.*

Dehydration is a significant problem on the planet. However, our liver steps up once again to adapt to this. Someone's exhibition of the symptoms of chronic dehydration depends on their constitution. Someone's genes do not define a good physical constitution. Instead, it involves having fewer toxins in the body which make for stronger organs and fewer poor health conditions. Hence, more toxins in the body will produce a weak constitution. This leads to hurting organs, and the presence of poorer health conditions.

It is possible to feel fine despite suffering from chronic dehydration. There may not be any symptoms of a known liver problem or a low-grade viral or bacterial condition that dehydration can worsen. There may be an absence of allergies or migraines. However, it doesn't mean that there's no problem. Also, chronic dehydration catches up with the body in the end. It could be a stroke at age 65 or a heart attack even though you had regular exercises every day of your life.

This dehydration is not a once-in-a-while type. It can cause a drastic blood sugar reduction. It builds up over the years while people are running around in the office, shuffling between classes or completing an errand. All these add to the years and years of amassed chronic dehydration. Very few people drink a liter of lemon water after waking up in the morning. This is a protocol that keeps you hydrated throughout the day. A celery juice or smoothie also works perfectly well for this job.

Just be sure not to allow the recipe to include radical fat from tablespoons of coconut oil, nut butter, or whey protein powder, as those are all dehydrating. In fact, there should be barely any fruit. Traditional breakfast foods such as eggs, bacon, with a glass of milk or orange juice are also dehydrating. As a result of this, our livers have to adapt to never getting adequate hydration. This is what I call the camel effect. It keeps our bodies hydrated in the long term in an arrangement that is not perfect or ideal but contributes to life sustenance.

Lack of hydration results in the creation of dirty blood, a term for blood that is thick and filled with a lot of toxins and other harmful substances. Some people begin to have energy issues, and this is way different from fatigue. Energy issues are peculiar to people at the beginning stages of sluggish liver. These are people who used to be brimming with energy and could exert their muscles for long, however, their strength began to dwindle as they experienced dirty blood syndrome and as their livers started to dehydrate. Other symptoms of dirty blood include dark under-eye circles, Raynaud's Syndrome, gout, varicose veins, inflammation, and insomnia.

CHAPTER 11: FATTY LIVER

Key Takeaways

- *The body requires healthy food for its daily activities.*
- *The thickness of the blood determines if a person develops a fatty liver.*
- *The thicker the blood, the lower the oxygen present in it.*
- *The liver has difficulty breathing when there is little oxygen in the blood.*
- *Fat is the cause of a fatty liver not sugar.*

We all cannot do without food in our lives. It is as important to our existence as the air we breathe. However, we do not need just food; we need healthy food. Lots of things hinder us from healthy eating. They include; a busy schedule, a tight budget, increasing pressure owing to high expectations at work and so on. We often find ourselves resorting to fast foods and sweetened junks to keep up with the daily hustle and bustle of life. Our cravings are valid in the sense that these foods afford us temporary pleasure – precisely what we need for the daily stress that we go through.

Let us now imagine a case where we are more aware of food, less occupied, and with extra time to take care of ourselves. It could also be that you are blessed enough and have the resources to search for alternative ways of eating. We may find a diet that is not traditional yet incredibly healthy. We will be less drawn to sweetened junk food. We will search for thinner cuts of meat and remove grains and processed foods. Shouldn't this work? Not exactly, if the aim is avoiding a fatty liver. Modern fashionable diets would still not appeal much to your liver.

Our liver's primary function is collecting a clean, filtered, tested, measured blood in large streams. This is what enables it to carry out the next 2,000 chemical functions. Now, the liver's primary concern is the thickness of your blood. It is the thickness of your blood that determines whether you develop a fatty (or pre-fatty) liver. The content of the depth is responsible for how fast you'll develop a fatty liver.

You might be wondering why blood thickness is the principal factor. The reason is that the thicker the blood, the lesser the chance of oxygen staying in it. The presence of less oxygen in the blood that goes to the liver makes it difficult for the liver to breathe. It is true that your liver breathes. The liver can be viewed as a set of lungs, the left lobe as the left lung and the right lobe as the right lung. Another way to envisage the liver is as a sea urchin living in the depths of the ocean, extracting oxygen from the sea water. The toxic particles being held by the liver causes it to have difficulty breathing. This weakens the life force of the liver. Just the same way you find breathing difficult in a polluted environment is the way your liver cannot stand the polluted content of your blood.

Doctors should intensify research on fatty livers, its avoidable causes, and disastrous consequences. This will make detection of liver damage easy so that a routine checkup at the hospital should see a doctor questioning a patient on the kinds of food he eats regularly. The doctor is also able to see and make his patient realize that a blood test reveals the high level of fat in his bloodstream. This then leads to the doctor advising the patient against having such a fatty diet. The doctor goes on to proffer the necessary foods the patient should take to prevent a liver breakdown, illnesses, and diseases.

Fruits also play an important role in maintaining a healthy diet. Sugar should not be blamed as the cause of a fatty liver. This is because it is always eaten with fat. Fat is the actual problem. The river of blood that enters the liver from the digestive system is already lower in oxygen. This is why less oxygen makes a big difference to the liver. Majority of the blood entering through the hepatic portal vein is full of toxins, pathogens, etc. This is why it needs to be filtered and processed. The fact is this; our livers play a pivotal role in the overall wellbeing of our body. Regular exercises, popular diets, and regular visits to the hospital are not enough in preventing a fatty liver. A drastic reduction of intake of fatty foods will also go a long way.

CHAPTER 12: WEIGHT GAIN

Key Takeaways

- *The liver, not slow metabolism, plays a significant role in weight gain.*

- *A thyroid problem does not cause weight gain.*

- *Viral activity such as excess waste matter damages the liver.*

- *Weight gain happens when the liver has too much to store.*

- *A liver loaded with excess fat or toxins fosters weight gain.*

There are some common reasons for weight gain often given by health and fitness professionals. Slow metabolism is one. Eating too much is another. Often times, you hear the same thing- too many carbs, lack of regular exercise, etc- so much that you wonder if there's any way out . You've done all that is asked of you, yet there's no improvement. People who are overweight or obese often suffer shame and low self-esteem.

However, what many do not know is that there is something called mystery weight gain. It has nothing to do with the reasons mentioned above. The way the body gains or loses weight is a mystery in the medical field. There is no such thing as a slow metabolism. Metabolism is nothing more than the ancient knowledge that the body assimilates food and uses it for energy. Telling people that they have a slow metabolism causes despair more than relief.

Most often than not, the liver has a significant role to play in weight gain. The involvement of the thyroid and the adrenals cannot be undermined, but we must also realize that both of them lead back to the liver. While it is fashionable now to attribute weight to the thyroid, it should be known that a thyroid problem does not cause weight gain. In the U.S., there are thousands of people who have a thyroid disorder and are not overweight.

Metabolism is only a myth believed to cause weight gain. Thyroid doesn't cause weight gain. The cases of people who are overweight and diagnosed with a thyroid disorder are nothing but a mere coincidence. The reason thyroid is linked with weight gain is because it is believed to be the body's metabolism regulator. Medical research and science do not fully understand how the thyroid works.

Thyroid issues are viral over 95 percent of the time. Chronic viral infections weaken and burden the liver. This is partly because the virus that causes thyroid problems nests in the liver on its way to the thyroid. The liver gets damaged by viral activity; it gets overloaded with its waste matter. So the filtering process cannot be adequately carried out, eventually leading to weight gain. The adrenal glands are becoming more relevant in today's medical science and research. This is good news. It shows the commitment of medical practitioners to the intricacies of the human body. These committed and kind-hearted practitioners deserve accolades for devoting time and resources to looking for ideas that are beneficial to the wellbeing of their patients.

The adrenals are not yet fully understood by medical science and research. We should be careful of attributing just about anything – depression, anxiety, insomnia, fatigue, etc. – to it just to satisfy our constant curiosity. Now, weight gain has been attributed to it. The level of excess adrenaline we are exposed to is what causes a chain reaction that can lead to weight gain. Weight gain occurs when the liver has too much to store.

The pace, at which your liver functions, either fast or slow, is what determines weight gain. However, your body is not to blame for being faulty. No one is saying you inherited a weak or strong liver. This is a matter of what your liver is up against. When a slim person seems to get away with junk food, it is because their liver has not been loaded with excess fat or poison which makes it function at a faster pace. Viral and bacterial damage also play a role. EBV is one virus that attacks the liver.

It is important to realize that being overweight is not your fault. You should understand that your liver can be plagued by all sorts – a viral infection, adrenal strain, and toxic exposure. Addressing all these is what indeed facilitates weight loss.

CHAPTER 13: MYSTERY HUNGER

Key Takeaways

- *Constant hunger is not caused by greed.*

- *A starving liver leads to overeating.*

- *Glucose and glycogen satisfy a starving liver.*

- *Pathogens weaken and stress the liver out.*

- *Radical fats in foods prevent the liver from putting sugars to good use.*

Constant, unusual, and problematic hunger has become a plague to many today. People who experience this mystery hunger are usually seen as gluttons or having a character or moral flaw. However, treating people who are seemingly always hungry is a wrong thing to do. No one is at fault for having to deal with a nagging hunger that no amount of food can satisfy. Many theories have been brought forth to explain the cause of this insatiable hunger. One theory claims it is a psychological eating disorder, and another suggests a brain or stomach disorder is making the hunger "shutoff switch" malfunction. There is also the theory that excess hunger is hormonal, especially in cases of pregnant women.

Hyperthyroidism has also been put forth as another theory. This is said to be when an overactive thyroid causes calories to burn faster than normal, and this results in people getting hungrier than normal. These theories are all unproven possibilities. The truth is, it is a starving liver that sparks off the need to overeat and causes mystery hunger.

It is ironical that a person who eats all the time has a starving liver. However, the liver is hungry for glucose and glycogen, not for fat calories. These glucose and glycogen reserves are replenished with critical clean carbohydrates (CCC). A pregnant woman's constant hunger is usually blamed on her hormones. However, thus insatiable hunger during pregnancy is actually because the woman's liver needs sufficient natural sugars to produce glucose and glycogen that will feed and protect the developing baby.

These reserves of glucose and glycogen once present in the liver get lost when the liver goes through overwhelming stress. Pathogenic activity such as viruses and bacteria in the liver is a significant stressor as well as byproduct and sludge from other pathogens, plastics, and petroleum from drugs. The liver's glucose deficiency to battle the Epstein-Barr Virus residing in it is the cause of the constant hunger associated with hyperthyroidism.

Glucose in the liver is inhibited by fat which are obstacles to its absorption. Contrary to popular belief, we do not get more glucose into out body than we do. Even though we consume a lot of sugar and carbs, the radical fat in these foods prevents our hungry livers from topping up its glucose reserves because the fat impedes the liver's ability to separate the sugar.

The best method for solving constant hunger and low glucose levels in the liver is to feed it with the right foods. Eat foods that replenish your glucose and glycogen reserves. Take note that alcohol does not improve your glucose level. Your hunger is a signal for help from your liver. You can rescue your liver by choosing foods that won't hinder glucose absorption.

CHAPTER 14: AGING

Key Takeaways

- *Aging is a significant fear in today's society.*

- *The state of our livers can sponsor either rapid or slow aging.*

- *Our livers hold the keys to longevity and staying young.*

- *Signs of rapid aging show up when the liver is not fed correctly.*

- *A weak DNA is the result of an overburdened liver.*

Everyone in today's society is afraid of aging. This has driven the rave for anti-aging skin care products, exercise programs, supplements, injections, and even diet programs. The desire to hold on to ourselves and our being as we grow older is embedded in every human being. However, we would benefit more if we focused our energies on knowing what makes us age than allowing false anti-aging promises distract us.

Several theories and truths such as the roles of your genes or stress have been believed to be the cause of rapid aging. However, the answer lies with one major foundational factor which can either age us rapidly or slow down our aging. It is our personalized time machine or fountain of youth, and it has been with us since even before we were born. It is the secret to longevity and the right anti-aging process. It is none other than our livers.

Your liver can backfire or retreat into survival mode if handled improperly or ignorantly. It will stand loyally behind you and only turn its back on you if you make it sluggish. When the liver begins to get weak and burdened, symptoms like saggy or discolored skin begins to show up. This along with other signs of rapid aging is inevitable if the liver isn't given what it requires to be in perfect condition to help you stay younger. Proper care of our livers will determine if we live in good health, look young, and remain balanced in our mental, physical, end even emotional well-being.

To avoid aging before our time, we must ensure that the liver doesn't take all the hits. Instead, we should take care of it properly, since it's the gateway to a young and healthy life. The liver's abilities to keep us young are mind-blowing. These abilities include the function of detoxification. By getting rid of toxins and poisons, your trusted liver is fit to work.

Your liver also has the profound ability to take antioxidants from fruits, combine it with amino acids and send them as phytochemical compounds into your blood to keep healthy cells alive. However, a hurting liver dies slowly over time from battles and wars, lifestyle exposures, and from uncontrollable environmental elements. However, the liver fights hard all this while to keep you young. However, if you don't give it the support it requires by replenishing its reserves with proper foods, its brilliant anti-aging ability begins to dwindle, and it focuses on just keeping you alive instead.

Our DNA has nothing to do with aging. It only reveals information about the state of our flawed livers. A weak, worn out, or injured DNA - which science mistakes for mutation - is a sign that the liver is gradually getting unable to keep us young. Our livers possess a chemical compound that keeps our cells from dying and this is the same antioxidant chemical compound that keeps our DNA from getting frayed or worn out.

CHAPTER 15: DIABETES AND BLOOD SUGAR IMBALANCE

Key Takeaways

- *The pancreas has relations with insulin production and diabetes.*

- *Medical research and science treat diabetes by administering insulin and medication.*

- *Diabetes traces its origin to our livers and not our genes.*

- *Diabetes begins at a very early stage of sluggish liver.*

- *A diet lacking sugar conceals a sick liver.*

The medical society hasn't scratched the surface of all the knowledge on blood sugar. Medical science and research relegate blood sugar and diabetes to the pancreas by making it all about insulin. However, many other causes of diabetes remain a mystery to medical communities. Even though the pancreas plays a major role in insulin production and diabetes, it is not the only thing that is wrong. Medical research has made breakthroughs in monitoring blood sugar and administering insulin and medication.

However, the real source of the problem has still not yet been found despite these excellent methods for handling diabetes. We must probe deeper into the underlying whys and hows, the reason for a rise in A1C level, the process by which insulin resistance is developed, why sugar is declared an enemy and how the actual cause of diabetes can be reversed.

The medical establishments are quick to heap the blame on a bad diet and lack of exercise when they cannot find the real problem. They also included the place of our genes as part of what takes the blame. This shuts the door of looking any further for answers when there are people who are prediabetic at a level in spite of tests saying they are. The origin of diabetes is deeply rooted in the liver. Hence, no matter how far at bay the symptoms are, diabetes could still be lurking around the corner as a result of worsening liver.

To help your liver, doctors advise a change in diet habits by avoiding unproductive carbohydrates, refined sugars, and processed foods. However, the problem with this advice is that natural sugars and other healthy carbs tend to be avoided in turn. Diabetes begins at a very early stage of sluggish, stagnant, or pre-fatty liver that escapes medical testing.

Fat, and not sugar, is the real enemy in the liver. Eliminating sugars from your diet may minimize the problem internally, but it will not be stabilized internally. The absence of sugar only conceals a sick liver. We must never think that our sugar consumption is too much and then reduce our dairy fat and protein intake. However, fat calories in the liver can be used up if someone exercises. This is beneficial to the heart as the liver's glucose and glycogen reserves are eventually transported there. Hence, a sick liver is reason enough for diabetes and heart disease.

CHAPTER 16: MYSTERY HIGH BLOOD PRESSURE

Key Takeaways

- *High blood pressure comes as a result of a heart, vascular or kidney problem.*

- *High blood pressure has to do more with the liver than the cardiovascular system.*

- *A clogged or stagnant liver causes the heart difficulty in pumping blood.*

- *Sugar plays no role in liver hypertension.*

- *Thickened blood and a weak liver cause the heart attack epidemic.*

High blood pressure doesn't just come along if there is no identifiable heart, vascular, or kidney problems. It is the same with how people are diagnosed with hypertensive issues without the root cause of it being indeed known. Medical communities resort to explaining the change in lifestyle, eating, and exercising habits for good. The patient is placed on medication if none of these end up working. Medical research is however ignorant to the fact that high blood pressure is more associated with the liver than the cardiovascular system.

Your liver supplies your heart with blood. When the liver is healthy, the heart draws blood like you are sipping through a straw. However, the heart drawing blood from a clogged or stagnant liver is like trying to suck jelly through a straw. This causes an inability to process and transport blood thereby making the blood dirtier and thicker. The heart will require more suction to pump blood from the liver. Harmful foods congest the liver and cause dehydration. This forces the heart to use 10 or even 50 times its usual power to draw blood to the rest of the body. This increased suction is pressure - high blood pressure.

A troubled liver is equivalent to a troubled cardiovascular system. Even when liver enzymes test doesn't reveal the problem, the liver still plays a role in this variety of high blood pressure which should be diagnosed as liver hypertension. Hence, clearing up a blocked artery begins with the liver. The sugar in your diet plays no role in liver hypertension. Instead, alcohol, as well as fat, salt, and vinegar, are among the major troublemakers. Excess fat thickens the blood, congests and dehydrates the liver. For people who truly live on a healthy diet made up of high-quality fats and free of salt or vinegar, toxins could become responsible for their sluggish liver. These toxins can clog the liver too and force the heart to raise blood pressure by pumping harder.

Liver care brings your blood back to healthy levels. It is highly essential that we take good care of our livers as this, in turn, takes good care of our heart and vascular system. Remember that the heart attack epidemic is caused when the blood thickens and the liver gets weak, sick, and burdened. Caring for your liver will not only replenish it but also keep you safe from vascular and heart disease.

CHAPTER 17: MYSTERY HIGH CHOLESTEROL

Key Takeaways

- *Elevated cholesterol problems begin in the liver.*

- *A weak liver has difficulty in producing good LDL cholesterol.*

- *High-fat foods contain the bad kind of cholesterol.*

- *The liver stores excess bad cholesterol to detox it out of the body later.*

- *A sluggish, pre-fatty, or fatty liver is what determines cholesterol levels.*

Cholesterol is not all about the heart and vascular system. A proof of this is how medical research and science has not discovered so many varieties of proteins, triglycerides, and lipoproteins. Elevated levels of cholesterol do not just appear out of thin air. It has a source, and this source is not in the medical communities' suggestion of the troublesome cholesterol our bodies create. Instead, high cholesterol conditions find their origin in the liver.

As the liver gets weaker, its original chemical function of producing good high-density lipoproteins (HDL) cholesterol begins to wane. The production of this good cholesterol reduces and bad low-density lipoproteins (LDL) cholesterol comes on the rise. Your liver is then saddled with the task of regulating and containing these bad cholesterols that can contaminate the bloodstream. Your liver cleans, holds, and controls them to protect you.

Your liver also stows away good cholesterol when you eat foods that are rich in them. This is in preparation for the day we choose to eat high-fat foods that contain bad cholesterol. These high-fat foods weaken and wears out the core good cholesterol chemical functions of the liver, and it is the liver's job to neutralize it. Our livers leave the bad cholesterol free-floating in the bloodstream to serve as a warning or alert for help. If there is an overabundance of these bad cholesterol, the liver is responsible for storing it in imprisoning containment units for the day when an opportunity arises to detox it from the body.

Someone's weight should not be used in determining cholesterol levels because a sluggish, pre-fatty, or fatty liver is the right basis of judgment. Someone with well-built muscles or on a good diet may still have elevated bad cholesterol or insufficient good cholesterol. The same way a thin person can possess a high cholesterol level. Regardless of a person's weight, if toxins and pathogens have been building up in it for a period, the liver will still get to the stage whereby it can neither produce good cholesterol nor store other fat and cholesterol, be they good or bad ones. With nowhere to go, this bad cholesterol ends up in the heart and arteries.

Hence, we must put it at the top of our priorities to care for our liver. Even though statin medication can seemingly reduce or eliminate bad cholesterol, it is only a manipulation as the liver is still in a serious problem. Hence, it is best to stop high cholesterol in its tracks before it becomes a menace. And if it has already become a menace, it is very much easy to reverse it. This happens by choosing the right foods and taking care of your liver with techniques that can revamp the whole issue.

CHAPTER 18: MYSTERY HEART PALPITATIONS

Key Takeaways

- *Ectopic heartbeat is a phenomenon that occurs when there is nothing wrong with the heart.*

- *Ectopic heartbeat or heart palpitations are hormonal.*

- *Heart problems have been around for a long time, but the mystery heart palpitations are new to us.*

- *The effects of the EBV contribute to mystery heart palpitations.*

Heart palpitations and other arrhythmias can be described in different ways. Ectopic heartbeat is one. It is something like an unexplainable skip in the chest that appears when there seems to be nothing wrong with the heart. Atrial fibrillation is another. A good cardiologist will often find the answer when a person displays serious arrhythmia. Mystery palpitations and fibrillation are also similar conditions. They have no apparent rhyme or reason.

Ectopic heartbeat or heart palpitations may be what you're experiencing if you've had strange vibrations around your heart and your cardiologist has carried out all necessary tests, only to find nothing wrong. Ectopic heartbeat or heart palpitations are hormonal. This is a mystery to medical science. It can be said that it is an electrical issue, not a hormonal one. Recently, the thyroid has also been blamed for this condition. In the case where a person has been diagnosed with Hashimoto's thyroiditis and also experiences heart palpitations, then the thyroiditis is said to be the cause.

Heart problems have been in existence for a long time. The mystery heart palpitation is what is new. It was in the 1940s that millions of people in their 40s and 50s began to experience these unexplainable discomforts in the chest. The reason that it happened to a particular age group at a particular point in time is that it was time for the viral condition they had carried with them since their childhood in the late 1800s and early 1900s to finally surface after the right amount of incubation time and the right amount of triggers. The virus had been docile pre-1800s before strengthening into a less kind force at the exact time that these people were coming of age. The virus, Epstein-Barr, is still very much present today. Now, it affects women as well as men in their child and teen years all the way up the ladder of ages.

The effect of the virus on the liver has contributed to mystery heart palpitations all these years. Another one is DDT. At the beginning of the viral explosion, DDT was also taking hold and wreaking havoc upon the liver. The risk of being exposed to DDT nowadays has reduced, but it can be inherited through the bloodline from parents to grandparents and so forth. There is also the rise of pharmaceutical and petroleum byproducts which had reached new heights by the 1940s and since then have had an increasing presence in our lives. These things reside in the liver and are attributed to mystery heart palpitations. They are, however, not direct causes of the mystery heart palpitations.

The beginning of mystery heart palpitations saw many people visiting the hospital. Mystery heart palpitations occur as a result of the DDT substance building up in the liver. It is not a spontaneous occurrence. It is something that gradually takes form as time passes. This substance, as it builds up, can make the heart valves stick slightly, sending the heart into a slight, less dangerous spasm which results in that uncomfortable feeling in the chest. This sticking is mostly caused by a diet high in fat, and the resulting thick blood. Fattier blood means thick blood and thick blood means dirty blood.

A jelly-like substance causes mystery heart palpitations. This substance is produced by your liver when certain troublemakers occupy it. A liver in good working condition should be able to provide a chemical compound to dissolve the sticky buildup. Mystery heart palpitations occur when the liver has been loaded with too many poisonous substances that it is unable to neither fight back nor carry out its normal functions properly. It remains a mystery to medical practitioners. And even you experience it, it's not a sign that you are unwell as any tests carried out on you may not reveal anything.

CHAPTER 19: ADRENAL PROBLEMS

Key Takeaways

- *Adrenal glands can produce 56 different adrenaline blends.*

- *These blends are produced by our adrenal glands in time of stress.*

- *Our livers are responsible for managing our adrenaline.*

- *Overusing detox products to clean our livers is unhealthy.*

- *The adrenal glands release lots of cortisol that help us take on life's challenges.*

Our adrenal glands can produce 56 different adrenaline blends geared to some different functions. This is something that medical research and science do not know about. There are the mild ones responsible for the everyday activities we engage in. There is a vast difference between the liver accommodating that everyday kind of adrenaline and the popular kind known to many. The latter is produced by our adrenals when we experience intense stress, exertion, alarm, and sorrow.

The second type of adrenaline makes our livers go through extra pain to protect us. This is because our adrenals must produce a potent brew of adrenaline to make us cope during times when we are suffering from betrayal, jealousy, hurt, pain, fear, attack, loss and other challenges that life throws at us. This includes activities based on adrenaline-rush such as skydiving and so on. The liver is wired to do the cleaning for us afterward. It is a natural process that gets us all the way through the ups and downs of life. Our livers surely do a great job at managing our adrenaline.

Some celebrated and promoted cleanse and detox products may, in fact, be doing more harm than good to our livers. Not all cleanse products meant for the livers are good for them. In the process of getting a cleanse product for yourself or another, you also need to watch out for the adrenal glands and not just the livers. Too much cleansing of the liver can upset and uproot too much. Majority of the cleanses nowadays are not good for the liver.

Adrenal glands generate serious heat. Adrenaline assists in keeping us warm when we are cold by making the heart pump faster and sending adrenaline through the blood at a higher rate to create the warming effect. The job of the liver is to counterbalance and soak up the hormones when there is excess adrenaline in the bloodstream.

It will interest you to know that a certain amount of stress and adrenaline is right for you. It is when there is surplus stress, an overload of adrenaline attacking the body that you should begin to worry as this can pose a much severe threat to the body if it continues. The adrenals are also releasing cortisol; when adrenaline is neutralized, cortisol can function adequately.

All the immune cells depend on the liver when the adrenal glands churn out adrenaline. It is the prerogative of the liver's immune system to be the strongest and smartest in the body, possessing highly intelligent white blood cells. The liver cells must be shielded from adrenaline to some extent.

The adrenal glands are quite useful in helping us deal with the challenges of life. They do this by releasing lots of cortisol. Our adrenal glands must be protected. Two adrenal glands are slightly different, as one is often stronger than the other.

Our body needs adrenaline, but as with everything else, too much of it is bad. The ultimate aim is protecting the body, so we should be cautious of what we allow to go down our throats.

CHAPTER 20: CHEMICAL AND FOOD SENSITIVITIES

Key Takeaways

- *A lot of chemical sensitivities are not obvious*

- *There are various chemical sensitivities, with some mild and others toxic.*

- *Your liver protects you from external and internal poisonous substances*

- *More toxins enter the body than exit when the liver works at a languid pace.*

- *An abundance of EBV neurotoxins causes food sensitivities*

Most times, people do not often understand people who experience chemical sensitivities. This is because the majority of these chemical sensitivities are not apparent to the onlooker. This is why many sufferers are often misunderstood and misjudged.

Individuals are prone to experiencing different kinds of chemical sensitivities. Some people undergo mild sensitivities and can cope with them. It is essential to understand that these people are not making stuff up; the chemical substances are indeed quite toxic. Some people who are already aware of their sensitivities still have moments when they are caught off-guard.

The first point is the liver. It has been vested with the responsibility of protecting you from external and internal poisonous substances. The liver is always kept busy with ensuring that you are free from anything that may adversely affect your body. Many people have livers that are working at a very slow pace. The toxins do not seem to be exiting the body. And they are faced with more toxins entering the body via food and other chemical substances.

Chemical sensitivities are caused by a sensitive central nervous system. Often, the toxins produced by EBV stored inside the liver cause chemical sensitivities. However, not everyone who experiences chemical sensitivities is suffering from a viral infection. Their bodies may have just developed a hyperawareness which is responsible for the hypersensitivity reactions.

An abundance of EBV neurotoxins is what is responsible for extreme food sensitivities. Sometimes, the food could also be a viral fuel. Those who have a hypersensitive central nervous system also tend to have hypersensitive intestinal linings. Lettuce is good for keeping EBV at bay.

Your nervous system might be too sensitive that even after healing, you could still experience reactions after being exposed to certain kinds of food. You need to know that you are not the problem; the world is indeed toxic enough. And these poisonous chemicals and constant stressors are the real problems.

CHAPTER 21: METHYLATION PROBLEMS

Key Takeaways

- *Methylation problems are not a gene issue.*

- *The liver performs the task of methylation.*

- *The ileum assists the liver in the process of methylation.*

- *Gene tests only lead to discovering the presence of inflammation.*

A methylation problem is as a result of the liver being too weak to methylate nutrients properly. Many people get template explanations when it comes to methylation issues. Most times, the genes get the blame. This has a way of conditioning many people to feel that they were born with a gene issue that cannot be fixed. However, this is wrong. People should not be made to see their bodies as faulty or unsupportive. And neither should they be told that their methylation problems are as a result of gene mutation. A methylenetetrahydrofolate reductase (MTHFR) gene mutation cannot be responsible for a methylation disorder. Many times, what makes us blame the genes is just a misreading on a gene test.

Methylation is the body's ability to receive, absorb, and assimilate essential nutrients that come from healthy foods, water, sun exposure, and fresh, clean air. Methylation is a job done by your liver every moment of the day, whether you're sleeping or awake. The ileum, which is positioned at the end of your small intestine, assists your liver in this job. In conjunction with your ileum, your liver alters the chemical structure of nutrients to become what your body needs the most.

The liver is left to cope alone when incoming nutrients are diminished as a result of poor functioning ileum. When an MTHFR mutation test reveals a gene mutation diagnosis, it doesn't mean your gene is mutated or injured unlike how science says it is. Science doesn't understand everything about the genes yet. All gene tests are geared toward testing for the presence of inflammation. It doesn't uncover its cause or what it means.

If your gene tests reveal that you have elevated homocysteine levels and issues around methylation, it could be positive on the gene mutation test. The negative aspect of gene mutation testing is the damage it does to people's mind and body when told they have faulty genes. An MTHFR gene mutation diagnosis should make a person hold on to the issue with methylation and not the gene mutation aspect.

A dirty liver and blood is the initiator of an MTHFR gene mutation test. This stage also reveals that you have a methylation issue because your liver is too weak to methylate nutrients properly. Methylation issues should be blamed on troublemaking viruses and not your genes. Your liver put in its best to battle these viruses and protect you from methylation dysfunction. However, it had to take up its life-or-death protection functions at the point when it became overwhelmed.

CHAPTER 22: ECZEMA AND PSORIASIS

Key Takeaways

- *There are over a hundred varieties of eczema and psoriasis.*

- *An allergic reaction does not cause hives.*

- *Mystery rashes and other skin conditions originate in the liver.*

- *Harmful pathogens instigate damaging skin conditions.*

- *Unwanted pathogens and viruses in the liver produce dermatoxins.*

Eczema and psoriasis exist in over 100 varieties. However, modern medicine seems to believe that everyone's skin condition is of the same nature. The situation accounts for the rampant wrong diagnoses offered when a person's skin condition goes beyond the narrow definition given to eczema. Rosacea, for instance, is also a variety of eczema, and not an entirely mysterious skin condition as is proclaimed.

Medical communities have also been wrong to diagnose lupus as autoimmune and give an explanation that your body is attacking itself. Lupus itself is a mysterious rash whose true identity has not been figured out by medical science and research. It is the same way hives remain a mystery being understood on a basic level as a rash-causing flurry of histamines. Doctors' medical training leads them to assume that an allergic reaction causes hives. However, these assumptions are not always right.

Mystery rashes along with almost every other skin condition originate in the liver. These conditions arise because there are unwanted residents in the liver. These strangers in the liver cause problems because they are the genesis of skin issues. They determine the type of skin condition that develops. Unlike medical communities believe, your body cannot betray you and cause inflammation by eating away at your epidermis. Hence, the autoimmune theory is an inaccurate explanation for skin conditions.

A harmful pathogen like EBV residing in your liver would pave the way for a more damaging skin condition. Different strains of the same pathogen have appetites for toxins that also differ. Therefore, when one strain of EBV prefers to feed on copper, another could prefer to feed on mercury.

The feeding activities of the different strains produce different rashes. While one could produce eczema, the other results in fatigue, hive-like rash, or a lupus diagnosis. As the EBV consume the foods they crave, the skin reacts by eliminating it. This produces a form of the original copper or mercury that is much more toxic and damaging called a dermatoxin.

Different skin conditions are formed by different types of pathogens in the liver. Copper and mercury combine with a virus such as EBV to cause eczema while three-quarters copper and one-quarter mercury with EBV is responsible for producing psoriasis. On the other hand, mercury is created when mercury combined with EBV resides in both the liver and the small intestinal tract. And this mercury also teams up with a higher amount of EBV to cause lupus-style rashes.

Skin conditions such as eczema and psoriasis build up slowly like chemical sensitivities. And they can make themselves manifest at any point in time. We shouldn't blame the last food we ate or our last action when they show up even though these do play a role. Instead, the actual cause lies in unwanted pathogens and viruses which reside in the liver and produce dermatoxins.

CHAPTER 23: ACNE

Key Takeaways

- *Streptococcus flourishes on food in the liver.*

- *Strep feeds on antibiotics and causes acne.*

- *Strep can adapt to the point of resisting any medication of antibiotics prescribed for us.*

- *Antibiotics can be passed down through the bloodline.*

- *Hormones are not responsible for causing acne.*

Streptococcus lives in the liver because it has an abundance of food there. The presence of acne means that strep is on a chronic, low-grade level. Strep feeds on antibiotics, which is the medication given to people with acne. However, there is one little problem which is this medication is harmful to your liver. Hence, a vicious cycle occurs as acne-causing strep feeds on antibiotics and the acne, in turn, requires more antibiotics.

However, Strep's incredibly flexible nature makes it resistant to the antibiotics that are prescribed for it. Hence, the strep in our body gets even stronger and stronger over the years as we move through various infections. From ear infections to respiratory infections to sinus infections, the strep becomes more immune to the antibiotics prescribed for treatment.

Antibiotics have always been in your body even you never had any prescribed for you in early life. Antibiotics are usually passed down through the bloodline, or they enter into the body through the animal protein. Strep doesn't just become resistant to these medicines, it also uses it as fuel. Even when you don't take antibiotics, strep finds a way to get the fuel it needs from antibiotics. It feeds off the plastic or even Generically Modified Organism (GMO) corn grow which are ingredients of antibiotics and the treatment for bacteria. Strep causes strep throat in children, teenagers, and even adults. The condition can lead to death as a result of ingesting highly antibiotic-resistant strep.

Hormones do not cause acne. Also, the suggestion that some cystic acne is autoimmune is false. Many people blame the hormones for acne because of acne's timing of happening during puberty. This timing is as a result of a lowered immune system during puberty. The strep takes advantage of this to escape from the liver to do battle with the lymphocytes. The strep cells are no match for the lymphocytes which is why they dash for the subcutaneous tissue.

Acne's development begins with the exploits of the strep. After forging its way through the subcutaneous fat, strep enters the bottom level of the dermis. The immune system of the skin fights back by gathering massive volumes of sebum oil to stop the strep in its tracks. However, the strep has enough fuel from antibiotics and can, therefore, fight through the sebum oil and survive the lymphocytes and killer cells underneath the epidermis. It manifests as cystic acne when it climbs up into your skin.

CHAPTER 24: SIBO

Key Takeaways

- *Our gastric juices are weakened by poor hydrochloric acid.*

- *Bile aids the digestive tract in the digestion process.*

- *Cluster minerals strengthen bile.*

- *Treating SIBO with antibiotics is a big mistake for SIBO.*

- *Strep is the single bacterium responsible for SIBO.*

SIBO stands for Small Intestinal Bacterial Overgrowth. Medical communities have been more than happy to use this as the newest diagnosis. However, like many of these other common medical research and science diagnoses, it remains a mystery as to its true identity. However, we must look to the truth of how the body works to unravel its workings.

Ineffective hydrochloric acid is a gut health issue that weakens the strength of our gastric juices. Glands and tissues in the stomach produce this hydrochloric acid. However, low hydrochloric acid is a sign that something is wrong with the liver. Medical science and research have not even scratched the surface of all that bile can do. Bile is produced by the liver, resides in the gallbladder, and aids the digestive tract in the digestion process.

The liver secretes cluster minerals in a filmy solution to strengthen the bile and keep it going as it journeys through the depths of the small intestine. Bile prevents fat from saturating the intestinal lining and going rancid. Pathogens are strengthened by feeding on these fats if they do go rancid. The result of this is SIBO or other gastrointestinal disorders such as irritable bowel syndrome (IBS), Crohn's disease, colitis, ulcers, and H. pylori proliferation.

Antibiotics which are used in treating SIBO are the biggest mistake for SIBO. Just like with acne, strep has been dwelling in the body due to inherited antibiotics or actual use of antibiotics. After years and years of getting exposed to antibiotics, strep adapted by mutating producing different strains and varieties, each of which is resistant to whatever strength is possessed by medications developed by research and science.

SIBO makes it impossible to identify strep as the single responsible bacterium. Doctors hit a dead end in trying to make a definitive diagnosis of the small intestine. This is because there are presently no methods of testing for bacterial overgrowth in the small intestine.

CHAPTER 25: BLOATING, CONSTIPATION, AND IBS

Key Takeaways

- *Production of bile by the liver makes for a healthy gut.*

- *A sluggish liver produces weak bile that has difficulty digesting food.*

- *Weak digestion originates in the gut.*

- *Bloating happens as a result of weak digestion.*

- *Weak peristalsis and inflamed on intestinal tract cause constipation.*

The liver's production of bile is the foundation for a healthy gut. The combined action of bile and hydrochloric acid in your stomach's gastric juices aids digestion. A weak and sluggish liver churns out bile at a low quantity and quality. This is a sign that your liver lobules are not fully in charge of their quality control job. However, the liver still does all in its power to produce the strongest bile even in its overburdened condition. However, there are liver functions such as immune system support which is more important than bile production.

Therefore, the liver resorts to lower levels of less powerful bile that encounters serious difficulty in digesting food. Food doesn't go through a proper breakdown because there are lower levels of bile production, lower bile salt content, lower hydrochloric acid production, and lower levels of mineral salts in your seven blends of stomach acid. This prevents the small intestine from absorbing the necessary nutrients and impedes the digestive function of enzymes in the small intestine. The totality of it is that there is weak digestion in the gut.

This weakness initiates bloating. In part, the bloating is as a result of the gut coping with poorly digested food and also a toxic-laden liver with contaminated bile that could end up in the intestinal tract or journey from the liver to the lymphatic vessels before being absorbed into the colon through its intestinal walls.

Pathogens feed on undigested fat and protein when bile and hydrochloric acid production is low. Decomposing food in your intestinal tract creates ammonia gas that causes your intestinal tract to expand and also allows the gut to rise into your stomach. This condition of bloating and discomfort further destroys hydrochloric acid, the tissue of the components that make them, and the stomach glands reserves.

Inflammation created by flourishing pathogens narrows and expands the intestinal tract in several areas thereby causing constipation. These pathogens thrive on a diet inclusive of wheat gluten, eggs, and dairy products. Other undigested foods that reached the intestines are also fuel for pathogens.

Constipation begins with the inflammation of the intestinal tract when peristaltic action wanes. The more weakened the peristalsis is, the more chronic the constipation gets. The condition is also informed by the extent to which pathogens are flourishing and keeping the intestines in inflammation. By helping your liver, you also improve your gut and heal any intestinal issues.

CHAPTER 26: BRAIN FOG

Key Takeaways

- *Brain fog can lead to loss of lives.*

- *BraIn fog does not originate in the gut.*

- *The pathogen EBV produces a waste matter called a neurotoxin.*

- *Neurotoxins contaminate the bloodstream.*

- *Harmful toxins such as mercury and aluminum can cause brain fog.*

People who have brain fog know that it is not an easy thing to overcome. It can be extremely detrimental to a person's health and vitality, and prevents many from achieving their goals. Losing a job or being unable to complete a degree are few examples of the detrimental impact of brain fog in people's lives.

Medical science and research blame the thyroid or gut health condition for brain fog. However, there are people with the filthiest, bacteria-laden small intestines and colons, yet, do not have any experiences of brain fog. If ever they experienced brain fog, it would be a variety that is so mild that it wouldn't even be worth calling it brain fog. On the other hand, there could be someone whose intestinal tract is free of yeast, mold, and other fungus and who is a regular victim of brain fog. The reason for this is that brain fog does not have its origins in the gut.

Brain fog is caused mostly by the liver and partly by the brain. Troublemakers in the liver such as the pathogen EBV feed on adrenaline which the liver contains to protect you from this stress hormone. Other favorite foods for the troublemakers include toxic heavy metals and pesticides. These food sources are in abundance that the EBV feasts on them to produce a waste matter called a neurotoxin.

These neurotoxins overflow into the bloodstream from the liver. They are very good travelers and infiltrators as they journey all around the body even to the brain. They tamper with short-circuit neurotransmitters in the brain and continue to be agents of brain fog in the blood and cerebrospinal fluid.

Toxic heavy metals such as mercury and aluminum are responsible for brain fog and creating a metallic runoff that negatively affects the brain tissue, electrical impulses, and neurotransmitters. Brain fog can also come about when troublemakers such as solvents, prescription drugs, and toxic chemicals contaminate the liver.

Other causes if brain fog includes a viral liver, EBV neurotoxins, adrenaline surges, toxic heavy metals, and other liver poisons. The gut is not among this list of the causes of brain fog. Brain fog varies from person to person and each one of these variations has its peculiar instigator.

CHAPTER 27: EMOTIONAL LIVER: MOOD STRUGGLES AND SAD

Key Takeaways

- *Emotional issues are not a hormone problem.*

- *The liver causes emotional issues in your body.*

- *There are many variations of SAD.*

- *Rheumatoid arthritis condition and sinus cavity sensitivity are usually diagnosed as a SAD condition.*

- *Weakened neurotransmitters cause focus and concentration impairments.*

When you're experiencing an emotional issue, it's standard to think you're being too sensitive or even acting strangely. We may blame the reason for our mood swing on being disappointed at something. Sometimes, people even think it's a hormone problem, especially with women. However, what no one has stopped to consider is that the real cause of emotional issues could be the liver. In the condition of a Seasonal Affective Disorder (SAD), gloominess, sadness, and unexplainable devastation are common symptoms.

Others can include mental torture, suicidal tendencies, low energy, fatigue, aches, pains, focus and concentration issues, and even a little weight gain. The medical community does not know the real cause of a condition like SAD, and in the absence of answers, they look for possibilities and excuses outside the situation.

Conditions such as a change of weather that comes with autumn and winter are often blamed. The SAD label was used by the medical industry to avoid further research into chronic illness and focus spending on other causes. Unfortunately, the medical community has not categorized SAD into its many variations. Had they done so, they would realize a deeper problem.

Some people have a rheumatoid arthritis condition that can progress from an arthritic feeling into severe aches and joint pain with all these from the onset being diagnosed as a SAD condition. Sinus cavity sensitivity is also a condition usually misdiagnosed as SAD. This is also the same as someone suffering from low energy for the last five winters which gradually culminates into more profound fatigue in the sixth year and is eventually diagnosed with Lyme disease.

The symptoms of SAD are explanations that the brain or another part of the nervous system is being affected by some deeper cause. And the season is not the cause. Inflammation of the tibial and sciatic nerves cause aches and pains. Headaches, migraines, tingles, and numbness are caused by the trigeminal, phrenic, and vagus nerves. Weakened neurotransmitters result in focus and concentration issues. All of these symptoms are neurological and originate inside of your liver.

Our livers play a crucial role in our emotional state of being. It fights to prevent you from being intoxicated by adrenaline in your bloodstream. The liver gets emotional when it is forced to let go of adrenaline that attaches itself to toxins. This is why you'll feel more emotional during the holidays. The liver has to deal with all the present-day holiday treats you receive, and this results in a mild feeling of sorrow the old body troublemakers are on the loose in the bloodstream once again.

CHAPTER 28: PANDAS, JAUNDICE, AND BABY LIVER

Key Takeaways

- *Our livers are already compromised from birth.*

- *Improper care of the liver worsens this compromised state.*

- *The liver and gallbladder cause infant acid reflux.*

- *A weak liver produces small amounts of bile and hydrochloric acid.*

- *Inherited liver problems can follow us into adulthood.*

When we come into this world, our livers are already compromised. Pathogens and poisons are passed down from our ancestors. The average person today is born with their livers functioning at 70 percent. Improper care of the liver drops this to lower and lower percentages throughout our lifetime. This reduction can start early in life and cause many of the mystery health conditions in babies and children. Newborns have conditions of gastric distress where there is an inability to ingest liquids such as breast milk or formula without chronic acid reflux.

The cause of infant acid reflux remains a mystery to medical research and science. Medical communities offer theories of the improper development of the baby's intestinal tract or stomach. There are also theories that reflux is caused by pressure in the duodenum because of the baby's intestinal tract sitting at certain angles.

However, it is the liver and the gallbladder that are behind a baby's acid reflux. This is because the baby's liver is struggling to produce its first portions of bile. These bile portions, as well as hydrochloric acid, are at small amounts because the breast milk is more of sugar and is very low in protein. The production of bile and hydrochloric acid at small portions is a digestive issue which is caused by a weak liver.

Another symptom of a baby liver is jaundice. In spite of all the signs, doctors still don't understand that acid reflux is also related to the liver. They instead present a theory that the baby's liver cannot perform the liver's normal responsibility of processing, dispersing, and detoxing red blood cells because the baby's liver is still developing. This is an inaccurate theory as a jaundiced baby's liver tries to overcome a high toxic load and function adequately in the face of conditions nor understood by medical research and science.

Most times, however, a baby may not need to have jaundice before facing gastric conditions. This is in cases where the baby has eczema or psoriasis. Medical communities don't see these as liver-related, neither will they connect it to the liver when the problems arise again later in life.

Children are also affected by pathogens inherited in the liver. A sluggish, stagnant liver can make children live life with unexplained constipation, stomach pain, intestinal spasms, and gastritis. Troublemaker foods like gluten and dairy and antibiotics also contribute to feed the already present pathogens and make the liver worse and underperforming. This, in turn, causes constipation and other intestinal issues.

PANDAS (pediatric autoimmune neuropsychiatric disorders associated with streptococcal infections) have symptoms such as tics, spasms, twitches, and acute attacks of OCD. Medical research and science have concluded that strep is the instigator of PANDAS when it is a viral infection.

It happens in children when they are exposed to massive portions of mercury simultaneously with developing a viral infection. HHV-6 is one of the main viruses that cause PANDAS, and a child's exposure to mercury strengthens it. These inherited liver problems are not genetic, and they can follow us into adulthood. The most vital thing is to know that the problem lies in your liver.

CHAPTER 29: AUTOIMMUNE LIVER AND HEPATITIS

Key Takeaways

- *Liver inflammation and hepatitis are related.*

- *Blood tests only check for the presence of inflammation.*

- *There is no easy route to finding out which kind of hepatitis is caused by inflammation.*

- *A viral liver is responsible for every autoimmune disease there is.*

- *Viruses residing in your liver cause autoimmune conditions.*

When doctors don't know the cause of illness affecting the liver or when treatment doesn't seem to work, they tag it as a mysterious autoimmune condition leaving out the possibility of it being hepatitis A, B, C, D, or E. The best they can do is label the condition as autoimmune hepatitis. But beyond the autoimmune label, liver inflammation is related to hepatitis.

However, there is no easy method to discover if the liver inflammation is caused by either hepatitis A, B, C, D, or E. Blood tests don't help much either as they are only used to check for any inflammation, blood disorders, or liver dysfunction. Hepatitis A could come into play if someone's liver inflammation has been long-term, becomes acute at that moment, and a scan reveals not much scat tissue. A critical and short-term inflammation accompanied by a slight fever, tender liver area, and an elevated white count could also show a diagnosis of hepatitis A.

A more chronic and longer-term inflammation that is not acute but has a little more scar tissue damage weakened white count, very mild fever and some on-and-off abdominal pain could be classified as hepatitis B. Hepatitis C has more scar tissue damage, long-term inflammation and elevated white count. Hepatitis D comes with a hepatitis B background when the liver has fibrosis or cirrhosis in various parts, chronic inflammation and swelling, bilirubin issues and massively elevated enzymes.

Finally, a case of hepatitis E is on the table if you have a persistent fever, acute pain in the abdomen, high levels of fatigue, elevated live enzyme and bilirubin tests, inflammation, as well as if you've been traveling a lot. If you've not been moving so much, the case then could have initially begun with hepatitis A diagnosis which could also switch to hepatitis E if you become much sicker.

A viral liver goes beyond just causing hepatitis. It could be a key player in bringing about any autoimmune disorder. The viruses residing in your liver are the exact causes of autoimmune conditions such as Lyme disease, celiac, RA, lupus, PANDAS, vitiligo, sarcoidosis, scleroderma, type 1 diabetes, Grave's disease, Hashimoto's thyroiditis, Guillain-Barré syndrome, fibromyalgia, Castleman's disease, Raynaud's syndrome, optic neuritis, juvenile arthritis, ME/CFS, polyglandular syndrome, to mention just a few.

CHAPTER 30: CIRRHOSIS AND LIVER SCAR TISSUE

Key Takeaways

- *It will take decades before the medical communities discover pericirrhosis.*

- *Pre-cirrhosis can be detected by imaging.*

- *Modern medicine is technologically limited in detecting pericirrhosis.*

- *Cirrhosis makes liver cells get damaged quicker than they are rejuvenated.*

- *The liver membranes prevent it from being hit by pathogens all at once.*

Alcohol and drug addictions are often instigators of liver disease, but we should not see view a person diagnosed with cirrhosis of the liver as one who has an alcohol or drug problem. A considerable part of our population uses alcohol and prescription drugs. Also, there's the fact that viruses reside in the liver.

However, drug or alcohol damage to the liver is not the cause of what I call pericirrhosis.

Pericirrhosis is a transition period that occurs in various tiny spots in the liver and goes undiscovered long term before the stage of cirrhosis. It will take medical research and go decades to discover this condition because it is undetectable by medical scans. Pre-cirrhosis, on the other hand, is a mild, early form of cirrhosis that can be detected in imaging.

Liver testing at present is guess testing. Hence, modern medicine is limited in detecting trouble such as pericirrhosis until it blows up and reveals that it has been there for years. Also, as the liver is not an important issue in modern research and science right now, no attempts are made to discover the foundation stages of the disease in the liver. This is why you must take up the role of caring for your liver. Otherwise, one day the hidden liver damage that has been building over the years will come crashing down.

Liver cells get damaged quicker than they heal when there's a condition of cirrhosis. A stagnant liver is packed with so many toxins that results in the formation of scar tissues. If the white blood cells assigned to the liver's portal vein and hepatic artery fails to eliminate an aggressive virus or bacterium, that pathogen can grow into a very radical one that can become unable to be destroyed and can cause a lot of trouble.

Some people may have a condition whereby scar tissue can only be diagnosed by the doctor when the liver is fully packed with troublemaking pathogens. There are protective membranes stationed across our livers that guard against these troublemakers crossing the liver quickly. These membranes are thin, fine, delicate strips that prevent the entire liver from getting injured all at once.

For instance, the liver stores pesticide damage to one area for it not to flood the entire organ. The thin strips of membrane create a process that prevents troublemakers from hitting the liver all at once. This is why cirrhosis can build up over time quietly and slowly.

The liver's safety mechanism contains damage in one area so that cells can continue to be strengthened in areas where there isn't damage. In other words, it prevents the liver from falling captive to the troublemaking pathogens in one attack.

CHAPTER 31: LIVER CANCER

Key Takeaways

- *Viruses feed on toxins to cause cancer.*

- *Viruses become cancerous when they are in a particular mutated group of strains.*

- *The theory that viruses cannot eat anything is false.*

- *Cancer does not just appear all at once.*

- *Hyper antioxidants send viruses in the opposite direction.*

Doctors think that viruses cause liver cancer. Although they can't guarantee it yet, they go with it because they know that problems such as hepatitis B and C are viral and can lead to the destruction of cells and cancers. It is true that viruses play a role in liver cancer. However, a virus has to be complemented with toxins before cancer can form. In other words, the disease is caused when toxins in the liver strengthen a virus. The virus must be in a particular mutated group of strains. This helps it become cancerous when they elope with sufficient toxins.

The Epstein-Barr virus (EBV) is a key player amongst the viruses that create liver cancer. There must be mutated strains to form cancer cells when it gets fueled by a strong set of toxins. Hence, having EBV alone does not pave the way to developing cancer. Other viruses whose mutations and undiscovered strains can contribute to causing cancer in the liver include the HHV-6; HHV-7; the undiscovered HHV-10, HHV-11, HHV-12, HHV-13, HHV-14, HHV-15, HHV-16; shingles varieties; and cytomegalovirus.

Some healthy diets are proof that we don't understand how cancer works. We must know which foods viruses feed on before we can say what is healthy and what is not. One of the biggest mistakes medical research and science had made is to think that a virus cannot eat anything. This theory which was passed down has now become law. However, this irrational belief prevents us from knowing how to tackle liver diseases such as cancer, liver tumors, and cysts. When medical research and science looks beyond this law to see the truth, they'll discover that viruses eat to thrive and cause liver growths, whether large or small, cancerous or benign.

Cancer builds up slowly and quietly not just appearing all at once. Your liver's immune system chases down viruses thereby creating a lot of traffic in your liver. A hyper antioxidant from an apple for instance partners with your liver and sends the virus in the opposite direction.

A mutated virus strain in the liver can cause cancer. Inside the liver, it continues to mutate by feeding on the right toxins. It processes and remanufactures these toxins to make them much more poisonous and then excretes them into the liver tissue around it. These more-poisonous toxins act as fuel for other virus cells they come in contact with until the virus cells are healthy enough to survive and multiply.

Therefore, to defend your body against cancer, you must protect your liver by ensuring that the pathogens in it are killed off before they get the opportunity to spread to the rest of your body. It is also important that you minimize the toxic viral fuel that strengthens any virus in your body.

CHAPTER 32: GALLBLADDER SICKNESS

Key Takeaways

- *There is more to the gallbladder than meets the eye.*

- *The gallbladder houses secrets of our battle with toxins.*

- *Food-borne pathogens are responsible for food poisoning.*

- *Medical research and science have come to know only two types of gallstones.*

- *The liver's bile is the greatest probiotic.*

The gallbladder sits beneath the right side if your liver and its job are to store bile from the liver. There is more to this little organ that meets the eye. The gallbladder holds a lot of dark secrets and mysteries that even the medical industry doesn't want to look into it for fear of what may be found. The medical establishment has camped around studying the gallstones and is not interested in digging deeper.

However, a further look into the gallbladder itself would reveal its many battle scars to us. Medical communities have ignored a deep pile of muck, debris, and sewage which they view as merely "sand." When revealed by ultrasound, CT scan or other imaging, it is ignored, and instead, the focus is shifted to more visible gallstones.

However, this gallbladder sludge houses a hidden story similar to the one that dirty blood tells us. A deeper look into the gallbladder will educate us on all the warfare we go through every day with toxins. This organ may seem small and insignificant, but it deserves our full attention.

Food-borne pathogens initiate food poisoning via bacteria and other highly toxic microorganisms. We may not know it, but food poisoning often comes with an attack on the gallbladder. This is because of the pathogens responsible for food poisoning travel around the stomach and intestinal tract and into the gallbladder.

Most often, the gallbladder is saved by the liver's production of very strong bile. Bile is the greatest probiotic, and a healthy liver equates strong bile with the proper acid balance and the right pH. Our gallbladders are weakened by the accumulation of stones, sediment, or sludge as we get older. This prevents bile from entering the gallbladder and exposes it to damage and infection from food poisoning. Doctors overlook this food poisoning and label it as cholecystitis because it seems only like inflammation.

Medical research and science are familiar with two types of gallstones: cholesterol stones and pigment stones (also called bilirubin stones). Pigment stones are created when the liver is going through constant toxicity. The liver's process of detoxification fosters the death of red blood cells which collect and stick together like a ball of clay. Cholesterol stones are also forged when bad cholesterol combines with the toxic matter in a liver that is overheating. They cool off in the gallbladder as fully formed stones.

It is a common practice to flush the gallbladder of these stones. However, it is unhealthy to down a large quantity of olive oil all at once. This forces the liver to use all of its reserves to produce an enormous amount of bile to send to the gallbladder for delivery to the digestive tract.

This is not a good idea because it weakens the liver more and more. A better way to keep gallstones from growing, dissolving them, and recovering and restoring the liver is with fruit. Fruit is not the enemy. You should lower your dense protein I take and introduce more fruit into your diet. A glass of lemon or lime water every morning and evening is also an excellent method for dissolving gallstones.

CHAPTER 33: PEACE WITHIN YOUR BODY

Key Takeaways

- *The liver performs over 2,000 chemical functions.*

- *Taking care of our livers is taking care of our bodies.*

- *We must take it upon ourselves to clean our livers.*

- *There are many liver myths that we must avoid.*

- *High-fat trends are not an ally of your liver.*

Your liver takes care of you like a baby. It has always been there from you even in your mother's womb. You are your liver's most prized possession. While in the womb, your liver received detailed, vital information directly from your mother's liver on how to perform over 2,000 chemical functions. It inherited a blessing from your mother's liver and a paramount instruction never to give up on you.

Many of the liver's functions are till date undiscovered by medical research and science. The motherhood quality of the liver is a never-give-up attitude even in the most trying and toughest times. Your liver puts in all its efforts to surmount whatever obstacle is thrown at it. It will take a bullet for you in hopes that you will one day realize that it needs to be rescued.

Taking care of our bodies goes beyond looks or a lean physique and soft, glowing skin. If we are not caring for our livers, we are leaving out the most important thing. Most times, we ignore our livers upon all that they do for us. Life's challenges and activities nearly drown us and that our livers go entirely out of our radar.

Also, there's no Liver 101 to bring to our remembrance the invisible power and all the incredible functions of our livers. There's no reminder from anyone or anywhere to clean our livers regularly. As a see-it-to-believe-it society, we ignore our livers just because which can't see the inherited toxins or the pathogens plaguing it.

Liver rescue requires you to have a lot of weapons in your arsenal. The first of these weapons is the knowledge that busts several liver myths. You must avoid these fads, trends, mistakes, and misconceptions. You must understand that the high-fat direction is not on your liver's side. Get to know the troublemakers constituting a menace in your liver and also tips on how to fuel and recover your liver with effective foods, herbs, and supplements.

CHAPTER 34: LIVER MYTHS DEBUNKED

Key Takeaways

- *Liver myths do not help us in any way.*

- *The time it takes for all body cells to be recreated is a mystery.*

- *The factors responsible for cell regeneration differ in each person.*

- *The liver holds information from past generations.*

- *Poisons and pathogens can be inherited.*

We must be aware that there are many liver myths out there. These are merely fads, trends, or even persistent theories and beliefs that are useless and not beneficial to us in any way. No accurate science tells us how long it takes for all of the cells in the body to be renewed, replaced, or recreated. This phenomenon remains an undiscovered mystery.

However, the factors responsible for the process of cell regeneration differ from person to person. The factors which determine the speed at which cells are revived include nutrients, stress, pathogens, deficiencies, inherited and newly encountered toxins, a person's environmental challenges and the resources available to them.

The liver's ability to hold information is so unique that even the brain cannot be compared to it. Intelligence from generations and generations past is stored in our livers. This information, as well as poisons and pathogens, are passed down to future generations. The liver is infallible because of this storehouse of data. Its ability to renew is more profound than any other part of your body even though it can't restore its entire self like the other parts of the body do. The liver's renewal process does not happen every day. It renews itself in thirds within nine years.

Another of these myths to take note of is the trend of bringing the bile from an ox and using it as a remedy for people with digestive problems. While this seems like a flawless idea, it is wrong. The human liver doesn't like it, and it is screaming for you to stop doing it. Bringing bile from another source into the body is problematic and damaging. It doesn't fix the problem of weak digestion, and it cheats the liver of its right to produce its bile.

Eating liver is another of these myths because many people love the taste of liver and there's a well-established belief that eating liver helps in healing and strengthening the liver as well as in building the blood. However, this is far from true. First of all, there is no utterly healthy liver on the planet. Also, just like ox bile supplementation, the contents of an animal's liver will not be compatible with your liver.

This would be infringing on the liver's rights the same way we do when we perform liver flushes. This is like thinking for the liver and acting in such a way that we know what is right for it. However, our livers know better, and we push it against its will when a wrong flush happens.

Another myth is that there are liver stones. The liver cannot produce its stones. What people call liver stones are a mistaken identity of our gallstones. The liver is too hot for a rock to form in it. This heat protects us from stones forging in it.

People may think you're fructose intolerant if your liver grows more and more toxic. However, buying into this fructose intolerance and malabsorption myth will cheat you out of healing your liver. What causes the liver to suffer is that viruses and bacteria feed off lactose from dairy. However, fructose is not in the same class as lactose. Pathogens do not feed on lactose. Hence, testing for fructose intolerance has never been accurate and will probably never be.

CHAPTER 35: THE HIGH-FAT TREND

Key Takeaways

- *All diet programs have the same concept of high-protein, low-carb diet.*

- *Doctors began to develop an interest in food with the rise of alternative medicine.*

- *Hybrid high-protein diets are the most common diets today.*

- *Many high-fat diets consist of low-carb or no-carb.*

- *Fruit is not the enemy.*

Diet programs today are innumerable, and each one of them seems like a remix of the other. They are all in the same nature and concept which is a high-protein, low-carb diet. There is no autoimmune diet. It is just another anti-carb, anti-sugar, extremely high-fat diet. High-fat is bad for the body and diets containing it are just upgraded versions of the original high-protein diets. Many of these diets do not offer the body the necessary healing foods it needs.

Conventional medicine brought about a need for doctors to get informed about diets and food. There wasn't much interest in them before except the knowledge that too much red meat wasn't right for the heart. Doctors now want to know more about food because they knew from their own experiences and those of others, that medical school did not teach them adequately about healing foods.

These medical professionals, inspired by alternative wisdom, began to blend leafy greens and green juices into their conventional diets of less processed foods and leaner proteins. Today, the popular diets are hybrid high-protein diets which are high in quality "lean" protein, plant fat, leafy greens, green juices, and veggies, as well as introducing a handful of fruit.

Many high-fat diets have low-carb or no-carb. Doctors have observed that patients' health declines when low-quality carbs in a diet go up. The reason behind this is the combination of sugar and fat; these two are always at loggerheads. Removing healthy sugar from your diet is not the answer. Radical fat should be taken away instead, if healing for an illness were possible.

People are beginning to see improvement in some areas of their health because of simple diet changes. Processed grains, junk food, and fast food are leaving the diet of many, but that is not all. These diets aren't capable of tackling autoimmune and other viral-related illnesses effectively.

This is because many people allow their fear of fruit to overpower them. Fruit is not the enemy. The idea that eating sugar leads to a fatty liver and that eating fruits is harmful to the liver is a false one. Because of this misleading and devastating belief, many have veered off fruit which offers good potential longevity.

CHAPTER 36: LIVER TROUBLEMAKERS

Key Takeaways

- *The liver is divided into three general levels.*

- *The liver contains and releases troublemakers within these levels.*

- *The liver contains the worst toxins deep in its core.*

- *Petrochemicals are incredibly toxic to the central nervous system.*

The liver consists of two main lobes which are divided into three general levels: its perimeter surface, its subsurface, and its deep inner core. These three levels are the basis for understanding how the liver contains and releases troublemakers. These troublemakers reside in only one of the two levels of the liver, although, there are some that can spread out across all three.

A troublemaker in more than one level is in different concentrations or strengths. However, chemical fertilizers, DDT and other pesticides, herbicides, and fungicides are exceptions to this as they reside in all three levels of the liver in equally high concentrations. The liver tries its very best to contain as many of these troublemakers as possible in its core.

The deeper the troublemakers in our liver, the better this vital organ can eliminate them later on and protect us. However, the presence of fat and adrenaline in the liver with those troublemakers buried within is a dangerous combination. You must come to understand where each troublemaker chooses to reside in the liver and how long they take to cleanse.

The first group of troublemakers is the petrochemicals group which is incredibly toxic to the central nervous system. These set of troublemakers are buried deep within the liver's inner core. They include plastics, gasoline, diesel, engine oil and grease, exhaust fumes, kerosene, lighter fluid, gas grills, stoves and ovens, chemical solvents, solutions, and agents, dioxins, lacquer, paint, paint thinner, and carpet chemicals.

In the chemical neuroantagonists group, the troublemakers reside in all three levels of the liver in equally high concentration. They are frequently inherited from one generation to another, and they constitute a severe problem for people with a sensitive nervous system and neurological conditions and symptoms. The liver releases them in small allocations and commitment will help you get them out in as fast as a week or two. T include chemical fertilizers, insecticides, other pesticides, larvicides, and herbicides, DDT, fungicides, smoke exposure of any sort, fluoride, and chlorine.

Problematic food chemicals group don't take a long time to be eliminated from your body. As far as you're giving the liver what it needs to send them packing, they could be gone within six months to a year. They include aspartame, other artificial sweeteners, MSG, formaldehyde, and preservatives. On the other hand, the problematic foods group is the first troublemakers that leave the liver. However, you must avoid eating them as you cleanse them from your liver. They include eggs, dairy, cheese, hormones from food, high-fat foods, recreational alcohol, excessive vinegar use, caffeine, excessive salt use, gluten, corn, canola oil, and pork products.

Pathogens are at the top of the food chain in the liver. The key to eliminating them is to get rid of their fuel sources. They include viruses and viral waste matter, bacteria, food-borne toxins, and mold. The chemical industry domestic invasion group consists of troublemakers that are all around us. The only thing we can do is to avoid using them in our own lives and work on eliminating them.

They include plug-in air fresheners and scented candles, aerosol can air fresheners, spray-bottle air fresheners and mists, cologne and aftershave, perfumes and conventionally scented body lotions, creams, sprays, washes, shampoos, conditioners, gels, and other hair products, hairspray, hair dye, talcum powder, conventional makeup, spray tan, nail chemicals, conventional cleaners, laundry detergent, fabric softener, and dryer sheets, and dry cleaning chemicals.

Our livers also have to be cleaned of troublemakers in the pharmaceutical group. They include antibiotics, antidepressants, anti-inflammatories, sleeping pills, biologics, regular immunosuppressants, prescription amphetamines, opioids, statins, blood pressure medications, hormone medications, thyroid medications, steroids, The Pill, alcohol, and recreational drug abuse.

In the toxic heavy metals group, the troublemakers spread out among all three levels of the liver and are commonly inherited. They include mercury, lead, aluminum, copper, cadmium, barium, nickel, and arsenic. Also, a prolonged overabundance of adrenal stress and adrenaline-based activities should be avoided.

CHAPTER 37: POWERFUL FOODS, HERBS, AND SUPPLEMENTS FOR YOUR LIVER

Key Takeaways

- *Sluggish livers can recover very quickly.*

- *The liver eats food with its lobules.*

- *The liver properly distributes necessary materials into the bloodstream.*

- *The busy nature of the liver makes it always hungry for food.*

- *Alcohol limits the liver's capabilities.*

Our livers deserve the best liver fuel there is. This is why we must be mindful of the type of food we eat. We must be more cognizant of junk food and additives and agricultural practices. Our liver can recover from sluggishness and weakness very effectively. We only have to make sure we feed them with the required foods.

The liver eats food using its lobules. This food is fuel for them to work and protect you. The liver is a very busy organ. It stores helpful and harmful materials. The useful materials such as nutrients, hormones, biochemical agents, and chemical compounds are rightfully measured by the liver to be delivered into the bloodstream. The liver also protects you by burying harmful materials in the deepest part of itself.

People who follow the high-fat trend think that the liver loves and needs fat because it is responsible for breaking down fat. However, you must make sure that you have the right balance in your blood to feed your liver properly. Pushing back your fat intake by 25 percent will go a long way in doing this. You should also reduce alcohol consumption because it prevents the liver from acknowledging, deciphering, extracting, and retaining the helpful material coming from the blood.

Instead, you should consume healing foods such as apples, apricots, artichokes, arugula, asparagus,

Atlantic sea vegetables (especially dulse and kelp), bananas, berries, broccoli, Brussels sprouts, carrots, celery, cherries, cilantro, coconut, cranberries, cruciferous vegetables, cucumbers, dandelion greens, dates, eggplant, figs, garlic, grapes, hot peppers, Jerusalem artichokes, kale, kiwis, leafy greens, lemons and limes, mangoes, maple syrup, melons, mushrooms, onions and scallions, oranges and tangerines, papayas, parsley, peaches and nectarines, pears, pineapple, pitaya, pomegranates, potatoes, radishes, raw honey, red cabbage, spinach, sprouts and microgreens, sweet potatoes, tomatoes, turmeric (fresh), wild blueberries, winter squash, and zucchini.

For healing and supplements, the best options include 5-methyltetrahydrofolate, alpha lipoic acid, aloe vera, amla berry, ashwagandha, barley grass juice powder, burdock root, cardamom, cat's claw, Chaga mushroom, chicory root, curcumin, dandelion root, d-mannose, EPA and DHA, eyebright, ginger, glutathione, goldenseal, hibiscus, lemon balm, licorice root, L-lysine, magnesium glycinate, melatonin, milk thistle, methylsulfonylmethane, mullein leaf, NAC, nascent iodine, nettle leaf, olive leaf, Oregon grape root, peppermint, raspberry leaf, red clover, rose hips, Schisandra berry, selenium, spirulina, turmeric (supplement form), vitamin B12, vitamin C, vitamin D3, wild blueberry powder, yellow dock, and zinc (as liquid zinc sulfate).

CHAPTER 38: LIVER RESCUE 3:6:9

Key Takeaways

- *The state of your liver determines how healthy you are and will be.*

- *The Liver Rescue Morning can be tried anytime.*

- *The Liver Rescue 3:6:9 plan runs for 9 days.*

- *Drinking lemon or lime water on an empty stomach in the morning helps you flush out toxic waste in your blood.*

Every day, the liver is weighed down by fats, pathogenic activity and exposure to toxins. Your liver wants to be relieved of this burden. Relief from the symptoms of troublemakers will bring you the clear skin or mood stabilization or weight loss or lifting of fatigue you've been looking for. Much of your overall health rests on your liver condition.

You have to take the task of bringing your liver back from the years of unintentional damage that the organ has experienced. You will have to partner with your liver by cleaning it properly and effectively. This chapter gives you the Liver Rescue Morning (a quick, easy cleanse you can try anytime) and the Liver Rescue 3:6:9 (a nine-day liver healing plan like no other). These plans are effective, they have a clear understanding of how the Liver works, and they give it exactly what it wants and needs.

The Liver Rescue Morning and the Liver Rescue 3:6:9 is not another plan with an agenda. You need to shed some of your food belief systems to move forward with it. This is not a propaganda diet, and it is not trying to compete with other menus or concepts either. The Liver Rescue Morning and the Liver Rescue 3:6:9 are here to save your adrenals, nourish your body, and cleanse your liver way better than any other method you've ever tried. You'll be released from the box of any food belief system that has had you enclosed in the past.

Your liver goes to bed at the same time as you and wakes up a little bit earlier to do some housecleaning.

It cleanses and scrubs up the mess of the previous day. You should align with your liver's activities by getting hydrated when you wake up. Flush out toxins and waste in your blood by drinking lemon or lime water, celery juice, or cucumber juice on an empty stomach in the morning. The Liver Rescue Morning helps you detox when you hydrate well in the morning and avoid consuming radical fats before lunchtime.

You could also supercharge your Liver Rescue Morning by taking hydrobioactive water, which hydrates your cells better than a plain old glass of water can. It is best to save your servings of protein for later in the day as these impede your liver's detox process. Make sure to replenish your blood sugar with a little snack when you feel hungry every couple of hours. Avoid radical fats in the morning and focus on fresh glucose-rich fruits instead to fill your glucose and glycogen reserves. It is also good to avoid caffeine and processed foods during your Liver Rescue Morning.

For people with severe hypersensitivities and digestive problems, I recommend you try mono-eating and not the Liver Rescue 3:6:9. Mono eating involves eating snacks and meals of only one food at a time. The Liver Rescue 3:6:9 however, is a nine-day eating plan made up of three-day increments that gradually adjust your liver to getting relieved.

The Liver Rescue 3:6:9 begins with a three-day preparation phase named "The 3." In this phase, your liver gets to prepare for what's coming and to benefit from the events that follow. The next three days are comprise a phase called "The 6." Here, internal cleansing begins, and your liver starts to release the toxic waste it had stored for months. The final three days is known as The 9. This stage rounds off the Liver Rescue 3:6:9 and your liver gets to let go of a myriad of troublemakers that are released into your bloodstream for delivery out of your body.

CHAPTER 39: LIVER RESCUE RECIPES

Key Takeaways

- *The liver rescue recipe is made up of powerful healing foods.*

- *You can combine juice recipes to get your most preferred taste.*

- *The fat-free Orange "Vinaigrette" Dressing can be added to your liver rescue salad for a great lunch.*

- *Dessert options include peach ginger sorbet and baked apple roses.*

The liver rescue recipes consist of all the powerful healing foods that will flush away your troublemakers and recover your liver from sluggishness. The first group of foods consist of juices, teas, and broth. You can tweak juices to get your favorite taste combinations. For instance, the recipe for a mix of **dandelion greens or radishes** includes:

- 2 apples

- 2 cups coarsely chopped pineapple

- 1-inch ginger

- 1 bunch celery

- 1 cup loosely packed parsley

Optional additions to this include: 1 cup sprouts, 4 small radishes, and 1 cup loosely packed dandelion greens.

For the **hibiscus lemonade**, you will need:

- 4 cups water (divided)

- 2 teaspoons dried hibiscus

- Half a cup fresh lemon juice

- 4 tablespoons raw honey

Lime water only requires you to squeeze the juice of 2 limes into 2 cups of water. Cranberry water is easy to make also. You need:

- 4 cups water

- 1 cup fresh cranberries

- 3 tablespoons lime juice

- 2 tablespoons raw honey

Liver Rescue tea can be made in the morning and kept in the refrigerator so you can have it warm or cold all day. It requires:

- 2 cups water

- 1 teaspoon dried burdock root

- 1 teaspoon dried red clover

- 1 teaspoon dried dandelion

- 1 teaspoon dried nettle leaves

- 2 teaspoons raw honey (optional)

For your breakfast, the **watermelon slushy** is a great way to start your morning. It requires:

- 2 cups fresh watermelon cubes

- 2 cups frozen watermelon cubes

- 1 lime (juiced)

You could also have caramel apple rings which are made with 1 lemon (juiced and divided), 3 red apples, 1 cup Medjool dates (pitted), 1-inch vanilla bean (optional), and half a cup of water.

The **liver rescue salad** will be a great option for lunch. There are two available options, and if the fat-free Orange "Vinaigrette" Dressing is added, it's sure to spice things up and become a staple in your kitchen.

The first option involves:

- 3 cups chopped tomatoes

- 1 cucumber (sliced)

- 1 cup chopped celery

- 1 cup chopped cilantro (optional)

- Half cup of chopped parsley (optional)

- Half cup of chopped scallion (optional)

- 8 cups any variety of leafy greens

- 1 lemon, lime, or orange (juiced)

The second salad option can be made with 2 cups thinly sliced red cabbage, 1 cup diced carrot, 1 cup diced asparagus, 1 cup diced radish, 2 cups diced apples, half cup chopped cilantro, 8 cups any variety of leafy greens, and 1 lemon, lime, or orange (juiced).

For dinner, ratatouille has a very original recipe. It includes 1 large zucchini, 1 large yellow squash, 1 eggplant, 1 red bell pepper, and 4 cups cooked quinoa (optional). The tomato sauce includes 4 tomatoes (roughly diced), 1 yellow onion (roughly diced), 4 minced garlic cloves, two tablespoons tomato paste, half teaspoon sea salt, half teaspoon dried basil, half teaspoon poultry seasoning, and 1/8 teaspoon curry powder.

For snacks, the potato bruschetta is a great choice. It is made with 2 large or 4 small russet potatoes, 2 cups diced cherry or grape tomatoes, 2 minced garlic cloves, 5 fresh basil leaves (minced), 1/4 teaspoon sea salt, half of a lemon (juiced), and 1 teaspoon honey (optional).

The peach ginger sorbet is an excellent choice for dessert. It is made with 1 thumb knuckle-sized piece of ginger (peeled), 4 cups frozen sliced peaches, 1 tablespoon Meyer lemon juice, 1 tablespoon raw honey, and half a cup of water. Or you could have baked apple roses. The recipe includes 4 red apples, 4 tablespoons maple syrup (divided), 1 tablespoon fresh lemon juice, and 1/4 teaspoon cinnamon (divided).

CHAPTER 40: LIVER RESCUE MEDITATIONS

Key Takeaways

- *Liver Rescue meditations activate the healing process in our livers.*

- *Music is an excellent accompaniment while meditating.*

- *You can choose to end your meditation whenever you want to.*

- *These meditations clean our livers and assist it in functioning optimally*

We must discard the lousy habit of neglecting our livers. For an organ that does so much yet is appreciated so little, we must take a moment to tune into our livers in meditation. These meditations are serious stuff; they are effective and contribute to activating healing in the liver.

Music can be a great accompaniment to the meditations. Playing music once a day as you prepare to eat, can put your liver more at ease. This relaxing music calms your digestive tract and reduces the conflict in your liver and aids the digestion process by making it easier. This meditation method gives your liver all the peace it needs for healing and relief.

Another method is to fill your bathtub with water that's at a comfortable temperature for you. Add one to three tablespoons of sea salt and two tablespoons of kelp powder, and float a natural sea sponge in the water. Once in the bath, begin to envision yourself in a calm and relaxing little saltwater at the beach. The kelp powder turns your bath into an ocean-like environment, and Your liver begins to identify the bathing tonic and recognize it as seawater.

You could also go for a walk at any comfortable speed. As you pace, use your breath to imagine that you're pumping oxygen directly into your liver. This paints a picture of your liver as your lungs being refreshed with all that oxygen. This improves circulation within your liver and brings about new liver cell growth for the recovery of your liver. There is no time constraint on the walking meditation. It all depends on you and when you feel its okay to stop. If you can't walk, then you can ask the angels you're working with for renewal of your liver cells. This is known as the Disease Reversal Meditation.

For liver cooling meditation, you'll have to talk to your liver either aloud or in your mind. Communicate with it as someone who is very close to your heart. This is how you show it appreciation, love, and support. Your liver, in turn, cools down and lets go of toxic heat that arises from daily activities.

A recording of running water from a stream, for instance, will do perfectly well in the strengthening bile production medication. But if you don't have that, there's still no worries. You have to lie flat on your back, close your eyes and envision yourself before a river or stream. Take a few steps into the water until you're waist-deep and start floating slowly in it. As you venture deeper and deeper, the water goes beyond your waist up to your ribs and covers your liver area.

The meditation can last as long as you want it to. As you get closer to the bank on the other side, the water begins to reduce, and soon, you're walking out of the water into the grass. Visualize yourself lying down in the grass and taking in the sound of the rushing water.

You can come out of the meditation when you want to. This meditation supports your liver with bile production so that it can assist in the digestion of fats and the building of its bile reserves.

CHAPTER 41: THE STORM WILL PASS: PEACE BE WITH YOU

Key Takeaways

- *Peace leads you to have compassion for yourself.*

- *The presence of compassion is proof of peace.*

- *When we take care of our livers, we control the peace within us.*

- *Every hardship is a storm that will pass away.*

- *Compassion leads you to feed others with the peace that you have.*

Learn to condition yourself in peace. The soul of peace requires that you have compassion for yourself. Find peace when you're sick by knowing what's wrong with you. Then, come to realize that your body never lets you down. Another way to find peace is to know what to do for your body to heal. When you know that a troubled liver causes you so much suffering, and you

160

also know how to care for your liver in the proper way that will rescue it, you automatically start treading on the road to peace.

Compassion is the soul and power of peace. Peace is not just an absence of pain, suffering, disease, hatred, violence, or war; peace is the presence of compassion. The world is always going to be in a state of lack of peace. We have no control over that, but we can control the peace in ourselves.

This happens by taking care of our livers which is the body's physical peacekeeper while compassion is the body's nonphysical peacekeeper. It is impossible to solve everything around you and control people's free will. Doing this is the surest way to live without peace.

Above all odds, we must learn to sow into self-kindness and self-compassion. Know that every hardship and challenge is just a storm that will eventually pass. When life's bad weather threatens our peace, we can choose to hold on to living peacefully until the trouble blows past. We have no control over life's storms which is why our free will doesn't reflect on the weather of life's storms.

The goal is to change others' worlds, not by trying to control them, but by merely being. This is the true meaning of compassion. You connect yourself to God the moment you learn to have compassion for yourself. This is where peace comes from. The true essence of peace is a feeling that is beyond this plain. It takes our breath away for a moment and wraps us in the warmth of sunlight, all of it bringing hope and confidence that only a benevolent source can bring and assure that everything will be okay in the end in spite of whatever happens.

With your compassion, you can pour this your bowel of peace into loved ones and others who are drawn to your light. This power within you is given by the Spirit of Compassion and the Angel of Peace for you to unleash the divine power that is locked up within you.

CPSIA information can be obtained
at www.ICGtesting.com
Printed in the USA
LVHW031415161218
600665LV00004B/599/P